T0028941

stroke of GRATITUDE

To all those who are providers and wonder whether God cares about your challenges and material wealth, I can say he most certainly does.

To my loving wife Pathma, and our children, Nishta and Triynka, my mother Savithri and our future grandchildren. I wrote this book for you all. Embrace things that seem hard and don't run from them, pursue what seems impossible. To my readers for deciding to share my journey. I thank you.

WHOLISTIC
HEALTH
THERAPIES

Contact information for Wholistic Health Therapies Pte Ltd:
Email info@wholistichealththerapies.com.sg or call +65 68419925

ISBN: 978-981-18-3157-7 (print)

ISBN: 978-981-18-3158-4 (ebook)

Ordering Information:

Special discounts are available on quantity purchases by corporations, associations, and others. For details, email info@wholistichealththerapies.com.sg or call +65 68419925

CONTENTS

FOREWORD   9

INTRODUCTION   13

PART I: A STROKE OF TRAGEDY

CHAPTER 1: A Day Like Any Other   19

CHAPTER 2: The Diagnosis   23

CHAPTER 3: Rest, Tranquility & Chaos   27

CHAPTER 4: First Steps on a Long Road   33

PART II: LIFE AS I KNEW IT

CHAPTER 5: My Beginnings   51

CHAPTER 6: Starting the Business   59

CHAPTER 7: Starting a Family   67

CHAPTER 8: Starting in Wellness   71

CHAPTER 9: Expanding into a New Frontier   77

CHAPTER 10: The Breakup   83

PART III: TRANSFORMED INTO A STROKE OF GRATITUDE

CHAPTER 11: The Plan you wish you didn't need   91

CHAPTER 12: Recovery is not a straight line   95

CHAPTER 13: A Turnaround   103

CHAPTER 14: Coming to Terms with My Condition   107

CHAPTER 15: It All Starts with Nutrition   119

CHAPTER 16: Disarming the Silent Killer   131

CHAPTER 17: The Power of Movement   143

CHAPTER 18: Planning for the Future   149

CHAPTER 19: Giving Back to Society   159

CHAPTER 20: Realisations   167

CHAPTER 21: We Are One!   171

ACKNOWLEDGEMENTS   177

APPENDICES   181

ENDNOTES   193

stroke of
GRATITUDE

HOW TO FIND
TRUTH, LOVE AND HAPPINESS
IN HEALING AFTER A HEALTH CRISIS

AANANDHA SHARURAJAH

FOREWORD

Dr. Darren R. Weissman

What would your life be like without the distractions of negative thoughts, fearful feelings, and that insecure voice that at times prevents you from being your very best? Have you ever considered what you'd do if you knew you couldn't fail?

We know from history that we tend to settle for mediocrity unless we're challenged. But the gnawing dissatisfaction that led you to reach for this book won't let you settle. I believe that by picking it up you're ready to answer the questions above from your heart; you're ready to choose to explore possibilities that would otherwise be lost. Congratulations! It's an act of courage to explore new avenues; it's an act of faith to acknowledge that you want your life's journey to be more than the day-to-day hamster wheel from hell that keeps you running in circles.

What I've learned from my own work as a chiropractic holistic physician (and that has been reaffirmed by my dear friend Aanandha Sharurajah's journey to gratitude) is that the natural state of the body and of life is one of peace, joy, and vibrant health. No matter how crystal clear your intentions or how strong your determination, anytime you respond differently—physically or otherwise—there is something deeper going on. How many times have you read a book, taken a class, or attended a workshop with the conviction that you'd change your life, only to find yourself stuck again a few weeks later? Why does this keep happening? The answer actually lies in your subconscious mind.

The primary function of the subconscious mind—the reactive mind—is survival based upon protection and learning. One of the amazing jobs that the subconscious mind keeps track of is the regulation of all of our body's functions. These functions range from blood pressure, hormones, immunity, digestion, detoxification, muscle tone, cellular regeneration, and ageing.

As part of its regulatory focus, the subconscious mind also protects us from emotional experiences that are perceived to be too painful, scary, or stressful to handle in a given moment. The reactive nature of the subconscious mind means it neither chooses nor judges in any creative or logical way…it simply reacts.

From moment to moment, thoughts, feelings, body functions, and relationships are all at the mercy of the reactive field of the subconscious. This invisible system influences, directs, and orchestrates each and every biological and behavioural expression of health. When we are unable to process the emotions of a given moment, the subconscious mind acts like a safety valve, inhibiting processing or integration of perceived traumatic experiences. The result is that our abilities to heal, learn, grow, and evolve are directly impacted.

One of the intriguing aspects of the brain and body is that they're unable to discern the difference between memory, reality, and imagination. Beliefs—which are stored in the energy field of the subconscious mind— are learned and become 'looping programmes' that directly influence our ability to own our power and perceive life in the present moment.

When activated, limiting beliefs directly impact the emotional, biochemical, structural, and spiritual health of both our body and relationships. Simply put, misperception resulting from core limiting beliefs leads to stress. We literally begin to react as if the memories and beliefs in our subconscious mind are our reality.

Even though we consciously know we no longer live in the home of an alcoholic father or a verbally abusive mother, our brain and body hold onto these programmes and continue to react in a survival type of manner. The perpetual loop of this stress over time can and will lead to a complete breakdown in the integrity of the way we think, feel, speak, and act.

When you find yourself in a rut, afraid or unable to switch direction no matter how much you want to, it's those subconscious limiting beliefs that are keeping you in the rut. Being able to recognise limiting beliefs is a key component to transforming the perceived limitations hindering you from truly living a passionate and fulfilling life. And the secret is now in your hands. The subconscious mind is powerful; however, so are you!

To lead the path, we must first walk the path. In *Stroke of Gratitude: How to Find Truth, Love and Happiness in Healing After A Health Crisis,* Aanandha leads us through a portal to the next greatest version of ourselves. This book provides an authentic account of one brave man's journey to experience the power of the infinite universe and mind and, as a result, unleash the fullest potential of his body's ability to heal, regenerate, and be whole. Chock full of brilliant insights and emotional bridges, this book will open your heart, strengthen your mind, and align your actions in congruence with your most authentic self. If Aanandha can walk this path, why can't you?

Making lasting changes requires commitment, dedication, and a passion for bringing out your very best in each and every moment. If you're looking for shallow, quick fixes, you'll need to look elsewhere. *Stroke of Gratitude* will help you learn to live more consciously, to summon the courage to embrace those parts of yourself that you've been denying, and to solve the deep challenges you haven't been able to figure out. You'll discover ways to make important changes in your life, both large and small, so you can become the powerful person you were always meant to be.

Get ready to take the road less travelled: a path of practical and positive growth. Enjoy the journey—I know you will!

With infinite love and gratitude,

Dr. Darren R. Weissman

Developer of The LifeLine Technique® and Best-selling author of *The Power of Infinite Love & Gratitude, Awakening to the Secret Code of Your Mind,* and *The Heart of the Matter*

INTRODUCTION

About the Author

I am Aanandha Sharurajah (formerly Siva Ananda Rajah Retnam), a 64-year-old stroke survivor, and this is my story. *A Stroke of Gratitude* is the story of a journey back from the brink of death and the transformative powers of illness, hope and love. A stroke can turn your life upside down in an instant. Uncertainty abounds, and your mind inevitably becomes inundated with many questions. *Why me? Who am I now?*

At 55, I was flying high and running a chain of successful wellness businesses—notably Atos Wellness and Body Contours. If you have not had a stroke, you may think that this book is not for you. But I was just like you—living life and working hard to support my family. I started Atos Group in 1983 and then grew the group to be one of the largest spa and wellness companies in Singapore by 2011. I was the CEO of Atos Mayar Private Limited. Not only did I busy myself running my company; I did not smoke or drink, I ate healthily most of the time, and I exercised whenever I could. My dream was shattered when I was stricken by a devastating stroke on Tuesday, 3 July 2012.

A Gift in Strange Wrapping Paper

That devastating stroke took away my identity, my life, and my independence. It may now seem like something I could have so easily avoided and something that many may have warned me to watch out for. But nothing, nothing could have ever prepared me for life after that day. My stroke felt like a death sentence, but I grew to learn that it was not an accident that had come about by chance but by design. In reality, my stroke was a gift in strange wrapping paper.

I received my gift in strange wrapping paper in Adelaide in 2014 when I met Dr. Darren Weissman during the LifeLine course.

Dr. Darren put it to me so simply that I understood in an instant, and I accepted my debilitating stroke with a deep sense of gratitude. It was a gift bestowed upon me to serve humanity with this message of hope, a message that leads to truth, happiness, and healing. The seed that sprouted that day in my mind was to write a book that would bring hope to others, that would detail my journey toward recovery through acceptance and through rebuilding myself like the eagle rebuilds himself in order to soar again.

I was deeply inspired in an unlikely way by the story of an eagle. The eagle has the longest life span of all birds. It can live up to 70 years, but it doesn't reach that age without making some difficult decisions along the way. By the age of 40, the eagle's once long and flexible talons can no longer grab prey. Its beak begins to bend, and its thick feathers stick to its chest, making it difficult for the bird to fly with its aged and heavy wings. The eagle has two options: die or go through the painful process of change. That process requires the eagle to fly to its nest on the top of the mountain where it knocks off its beak by beating it against a rock and then waits for a new beak to grow before plucking out its talons. When the new talons grow back, the eagle plucks out its heavy feathers, and then, finally, it's ready to take the first flight after rebirth to live for another 30 years.

The soaring eagle

Whenever I wanted to give up along the way, that story motivated me to move from self-pity to self-discovery. I have learned how to look back at the past, and ahead to the future, with a brand-new perspective. Grateful for my second chance at life, I'm paying it forward by being an advocate for stroke survivors. I encourage all stroke survivors to persevere in their rehabilitation.

I've seen far too many stroke patients fall into a dark depression and resign themselves to the tragic fate of being stuck forever in a vegetative state. However, you have the choice to live an empowered life after a stroke. I am living proof that, with hope, it is possible to recover and thrive.

This story isn't only for stroke survivors. No matter who you are or what you do, you will reach a point in your life where you need to undergo change in order to survive. It might come without warning and when you least expect it, but you will have to pluck out your unpleasant memories, negative thoughts, and fixed mindset so as to free yourself from past burdens before harnessing a new mindset in order to fly once again.

I would like to share with you some of my personal insights regarding how I chose to live an empowered life after my stroke.

PART I: A STROKE OF TRAGEDY

CHAPTER 1

A DAY LIKE ANY OTHER

The calamity that comes is never the one we had prepared ourselves for.
—Mark Twain[1]

3 *July 2012: 4:15 a.m.* Another sleepless night, another day ahead. After much tossing and turning, I got out of bed at 6:00 a.m. to start my morning exercise.

With rays of sunlight slowly streaming into the dining room, I had breakfast with my wife and two daughters—as I did every weekday morning. That day, Sparkle, our puppy, had made a mess at the front door, so I disciplined him before I left. After our meal, I began the ritual of ferrying the girls to school before my wife and I went to work. I was 55 at that time; my wife, Pathma, was 53; my older daughter, Nishta, 18; and my younger daughter, Triynka, 17.

In the car, I took the opportunity to speak to Nishta about the importance of sufficient sleep. She was taking her A Level examinations later that year and, like many of our young Singaporean students, had picked up the bad habit of burning the midnight oil. To her, my advice probably came across as just another routine nag on another regular day. The day had started like any other Tuesday—and yet, when the sun set again, life would have taken a 180-degree turn for my family and me.

It was the third of July 2012, the last time in a long time that she would hear me string a complete sentence together.

Being the CEO and owner of several companies meant that I had to put myself out there regularly for long periods.

I glanced at my schedule. The workday was packed with meetings and other tasks that needed to be attended to. My last meeting that day was with my studio managers. The usual weekly morning meeting with my managers at Body Contours had gone well. I had come to find these meetings instrumental in tapping into the pulse of the business as they were the only chance I had to touch base with my staff, who were my eyes and ears in places that were not physically possible for one person to reach. Listening to their thoughts and ideas lent me great insight. It was my way of doing a health checkup of sorts on the business so that I could make better decisions with more clarity.

For now, the team and I were off to a brisk lunch at the nearby Windsor Hotel Café. But even as I made toward the car park to retrieve my vehicle, thoughts pertaining to the next meeting's agenda had already begun to seep into my mind like clockwork. In truth, lunch hour was never a true break for me. A perpetual sense of urgency permeated my waking life. I honestly couldn't remember what life was like before this, but I wouldn't have it any other way.

This feeling was particularly amplified this afternoon, however. I was due to meet my business partner later in the day for an important discussion, and it was one that might change everything. But first, there were pressing things to be done. I brushed the feeling aside. The staff were waiting for me to come pick them up from the lobby. Life, however, had other plans. I headed out to the third floor car park of the Cencon One Building to pick up my car.

The mounting stress had set off an invisible time bomb somewhere inside of me. And as I strode across the smooth cement toward my car, it dealt its final blow to my body. Hurriedly, I unlocked my car and sat in the driver's seat. As I unlocked my car and sat in it, my attempts to put my right leg in the car proved to be futile. Bizarrely, I found it too heavy to be lifted. Usually if I felt unwell, I would just shrug it off. However, I knew that something was seriously wrong this time.

With my consciousness leaving me, I needed to do something, and I needed to do it fast. My heart pounded in my chest, the beads of sweat forming on my forehead. My leg was like a tree trunk refusing to be lifted from the floor.

My consciousness was ebbing fast. The gravity of the situation began weighing in on me.

I reached for my phone and called my wife, Pathma. No answer. She was probably in a meeting. Thinking fast, I called Asok, our financial controller. He answered, thankfully, and alerted my wife, who set off to where I was at the car park.

Time was ticking. With every breath I took, I felt the energy drain from me. Pathma arrived at the scene with some staff and tried to get me out of the car. But the car beside my door was parked too close. My body had become deadweight and proved much too difficult to manoeuvre around the narrow gap between the vehicles. In the meantime, someone called an ambulance.

The air was thick with trepidation, a suffocating blanket. My wife and the staff grappled with their shock at how quickly I had been rendered immobile and inarticulate. Just moments ago, I was a completely different person who thrived on his mobility and ability to communicate.

Ironically, I began to lose control of my life and body in the driver's seat of my own car.

I soon became vaguely aware of several people milling about me. I could hear them, but I couldn't see them. Sometimes I would get glimpses of people for a while, but the world would go dark again. I seemed to be slipping in and out of consciousness. My breathing was the only constant, operating faithfully without my control, and was oddly comforting. It was so uncharacteristically quiet despite the scene around me; my mind seemed to have run out of words.

By the time the ambulance had arrived, I had lost consciousness and had to be carried out through the narrow gap between my Audi and the car parked next to mine. Unfortunately, however, the ambulance could not change its route due to protocol. It would seem that things were out of our hands until we got to our destination.

My wife later told me that I was first taken to Tan Tock Seng Hospital as per the standard procedure. One of the first calls my wife made was to my sister-in-law, Mala, who advised her to bring me to Mount Elizabeth Hospital—where she worked and where Dr. Tang, our trusted family doctor and respected neurologist, was. Upon a quick consultation over the phone with Dr. Tang, she was informed that we had a window of three hours. Meanwhile at Tan Tock Seng, a chest x-ray had been performed on me. With the help of Mala, my wife quickly arranged for an ambulance from Mount Elizabeth Hospital to pick me up, and I was moved so quickly that even one of my shoes was left behind at Tan Tock Seng. When asked, my wife lamented that in those moments she did not pause to feel—she had gone into a problem-solving mode that ensured that I was attended to in as timely a fashion as possible.

My eldest daughter, Nishta, had arrived before her sister, as her school was much closer to Mount Elizabeth Hospital. It was pouring heavily that day, and the roads were jammed. Seeing me lying motionless and unconscious had gripped her with fear. She tried to whisper words of affirmation in my ear, but I only stared blankly at her—not registering a thing she had said.

Naturally, to a young girl who was hardly exposed to medical conditions such as a stroke, this petrified her. She later told me that her greatest fear was of losing me that day because she regretted her last words to me—which were of nonchalance and dismissal of my advising her against working late at night. Thankfully, those were not her last words to me because I survived.

CHAPTER 2

THE DIAGNOSIS

A correct diagnosis is three-fourths the remedy.
–Mahatma Gandhi²

Back at Mount Elizabeth, Dr. Tang reviewed the CT scans, and he determined that a bleed had occurred in my brain at the edge of my basal ganglia. He immediately administered a drug to stop the bleeding.

'What caused the stress?' he asked my wife, as they looked at the scan results together. The truth was beginning to dawn on her. She had no answer for him, but she had one for herself in her heart, and she couldn't believe that it had led us to this point—the emergency room of a hospital.

The CT scan, however, showed no blockages in my system that could lead to a stroke. I was given some steroids, and an MRI scan was performed the next day to ascertain if the dosage was sufficient to arrest the bleed. The MRI confirmed a clear vascular system: my blood vessels were fine.

I learned that there are two kinds of strokes. About eight in 10 strokes are ischaemic strokes, which means that they are caused by blockages. The less common stroke is haemorrhagic, which is caused by a brain aneurysm or a weakened blood vessel leak that often poses a much more serious risk of death or permanent disability. This was the type of stroke I had just suffered, so the odds did not look very good.

On one of his routine morning visits to my hospital room, Dr. Tang drew a picture of the brain to show Pathma where the bleed had occurred. The haemorrhage had affected a portion of my basal ganglia and also the nerve pathways linked to the right side of the body. The basal ganglion is the part of the brain that is responsible for regulating speech, voluntary motor function, and emotions.

Dr. Tang explained where the bleed had happened

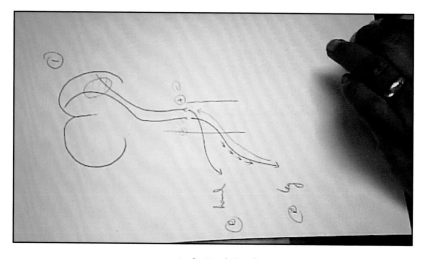

At the Basal Ganglia

The doctor's thorough evaluation of the area of my brain that was affected, as well as the extent of the bleed, proved to be vital to the chain of health professionals who assessed my bodily functions to work out a detailed rehabilitation schedule. These were the physiotherapist who treated my physical body, the occupational therapist who decided which activities would aid recuperation, and the speech therapist who helped me learn to use my tongue and voice again.

Since then, I have read many accounts written by others who have suffered a stroke. Some stroke survivors tell of a gradual deterioration of speech, movement, or cognition over a span of several hours before it even occurred to them that they might require medical attention. In my case, it happened without any warning whatsoever. It was so surreal—one moment I was in command, and it was business as usual at my office, conducting meetings; and the next moment, I was sitting in my car, immobile and unable to speak.

Barely two months before, in May of 2012, I had been told that a genetic test revealed I was at risk for a cardiovascular event. That confused me because I had previously had a medical checkup that deemed me to be in perfect health. It should have been a warning sign for me not to take my health for granted. I had not been exercising regularly, was under a lot of stress, and was making some poor dietary choices.

Sharon Palmer was a medical herbalist and naturopath from Australia who specialised in clinical genetics and who had set out to help me. Just weeks before my stroke, Sharon wrote down a list of pathology tests she recommended. The plan was for me to undergo tests, and then on her next visit to Singapore, she would review my blood results. At the end of the consultation, I told her that even though I was not doing all the right things, I was healthy.

Sharon felt that people tend to ignore symptoms for many reasons. Men are particularly bad when it comes to ignoring and minimising their symptoms, and businessmen like me are often so busy that they prioritise their business agenda over their health. We often think that we are immune and that nothing will happen to us, but the statistics say otherwise. Ironically, on the afternoon of 3 July, Sharon was waiting at my office to meet with me after lunch to discuss my test results, while I was in the car park below suffering a severe stroke that I was lucky to have survived. Still, my diagnosis told only part of the story. The more pressing question was, was I about to let the stroke permanently define me? Or was I going to define how the stroke merely bent the arc of my life?

I was not about to give up. Not without a fight.

CHAPTER 3

REST, TRANQUILITY & CHAOS

*Courage isn't having to go on—it is going on when you
don't have the strength.*

–Napoleon Bonaparte

My world suddenly grew much smaller and quieter. From the hustle and bustle of meeting people day in and day out at work, I was catapulted into the quiet of my fish tank–like room at the high-dependency unit where only two visitors were permitted at any one time. I hardly stayed awake, and when I did it was not for long. Soon, it became clear that not only was I extremely drowsy; I had also lost my ability to speak. Looking back at my life before the stroke, my biggest regret was not spending enough time with my girls, as I had always been busy with work. So, as I recovered, I was very happy to have their company.

 At that point, we were in a legal dispute with my partner, a great source of stress for me before the stroke. Although I knew I was facing serious pressures at work, I was happy just to be alive with Pathma and my daughters, Nishta and Triynka, around me. In fact, I was more at peace following the stroke—I was having a rest, one that had effectively been ordered by my body.

For three days after my stroke, I was drowsy and couldn't speak. I stayed in the high-dependency unit ward until the fourth day, when they transferred me to a room in the regular ward. By this time, I was awake, and I was aware that my body wasn't functioning properly. Because the stroke had affected my basal ganglia, I had no memory of what had happened in that first week. When I tried to move any part of the right side of my body—arm or leg—I could not move it at all. The left arm and leg I could still move freely. My facial muscles were not affected—I could still chew, blink, and turn my head.

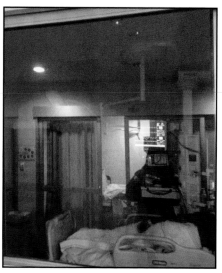

High Dependency Unit at Mount Elizabeth:
I thought it was a temporary paralysis, but
how wrong I was!

I thought it was a temporary paralysis, but how wrong I was! Gradually, the possibility that I would spend the rest of my life like this made my other troubles dim in comparison. I had never thought that something like this could happen to me. I had regarded myself as a healthy person. I kept asking myself, 'How can this be possible?' I had looked forward to living to a ripe old age—but not like this.

An MRI scan confirmed that the bleed had stopped. When the doctor was satisfied that it had, he arranged for detailed assessments of my speech and motor functions, including my ability to swallow. Thus began a series of tests to determine the full extent of the stroke.

Some of the things being tested seemed elementary, but they were urgent and necessary. It strikes me how we take for granted something as simple as swallowing, but in many cases of stroke, the muscles responsible for this complex set of motions are affected. A speech therapist also assessed me, and that information allowed doctors to determine the extent of my paralysis.

What I took for granted .. swallowing

The next day, my physiotherapist, occupational therapist, and speech therapist each visited me. Pathma diligently made a record of the various treatment plans they prescribed so she could learn how best to help me. The top priority, now that I was out of immediate danger, was to work on regaining my physical abilities. The other option was to accept permanent disability, including loss of speech. This was not an option at all—not to my family and not to me.

This period was crucial not only for my health but also for my business.

At the time of the stroke, my mother, who lived in Malaysia, my sister Ron, and my younger brother Sri all happened to be in town. They banded together with my wife's family to support my wife and daughters as the ordeal unfolded. Although everyone did their best not to show their sadness in my presence, the shock of the stroke affected them at a much deeper level. Some of the impacts were evident early on; others would reveal themselves over a longer period of time.

In the first few weeks, I saw mostly family members. Pathma limited visits to allow me as much rest as possible, and my mother and my mother-in-law prayed very hard for me. Once, overcome with worry, my mother ended up at Mount Elizabeth Hospital for a sudden blood pressure spike. Thankfully, it turned out not to be serious.

When my family had to return to Kuala Lumpur, my wife's family continued to provide constant support. My brother Sri, and my brothers-in-law Jeya and Maharaj, assisted Pathma with time-sensitive company matters and egged me on during my recovery. My mother-in-law made as many hospital visits as she could, even though she was not in the best of health. Viji, my sister-in-law, would enthusiastically encourage me to hum the 'Happy Birthday' tune to assess my automatic speech patterns. Gradually, I caught the tune and hummed along. Jennifer, another sister-in-law, gave me a DVD of the book called *The Secret*. I would watch it on a portable player, keen to listen to what it had to say about the power of the mind and how it could be harnessed to heal oneself.

As I emerged from the initial shock and began my journey of recovery and rehabilitation, I felt incredible relief—that I was alive and that I was surrounded by the love of my family. We became closer than ever.

With the doctors' approval, Pathma found ways to stay by my side as much as she could. She set up a small working space in my single ward so she could keep an eye on me and manage our companies at the same time. Her business meetings were moved from our office on Tannery Road to the cafeteria at Mount Elizabeth Hospital. Also, my daughters, Nishta and Triynka, set up a makeshift space where they could study for their examinations. During this time, my family, despite their busy lives, worked out a routine to ensure that someone was constantly by my side.

Alive with incredible relief

Behind these rosy moments, however, a grimmer reality still waited to be dealt with. We had entered into a major legal tussle with our business partner, and this had been a great source of stress for me right before the stroke.

Oddly enough, I felt a sense of inner tranquillity now—one that had eluded me before that fateful day of the third of July. All along, I had not thought to give myself a break. Now, my body had effectively ordered one for me, and I was finally being forced to take a rest. With this time that had been unexpectedly freed up, I was gaining newfound appreciation for the little things in life—even as the severity of the legal dispute hovered in the background.

About a week in, a surprise visitor came bearing news. It was my insurance agent, of all people. 'There's nothing to worry about,' Ashvin told me, even as I lay there trying to register his identity. 'Everything will be taken care of by my insurance company.' It took awhile to sink in after he left, but when it did, I regained some precious peace of mind knowing that at least one more obstacle was out of the way. It meant that my wife would be able to arrange all the treatments with the various health professionals and that all expenses would be covered by my insurance company.

During the first weeks of July, I received very little news about the legal dispute. Family and friends observed that I had made the greatest improvement in my recovery during this window of time, and it gave me some comfort to think that there was no pressure on the legal front.

At least, that was what I thought.

The reality was that disaster was impending. Pathma had been shielding me from it, but as the days progressed, the legal battle kicked into full throttle. With my mind now constantly occupied with thoughts of how to reach a solution, my attention was taken away from my rehabilitation and healing.

There were moments when I badly wanted to pick up the phone and call my business partner, who had initiated the legal proceedings. But at this point, I could not even speak. I was not sure what to do, or what I *could* do, until my speech returned, except pray for both sides to reach an amicable settlement.

All the while, I was so thankful to have Pathma by my side. She became a good de facto CEO, having effectively understudied me for the past 11 years since she had joined the company in 2001. She had much to figure out on her own as there were many things that had previously been only under my purview. Still, she chose not to discuss work matters in front of me as she felt that any additional stress would hamper my recovery. The close working relationship she had developed with our staff over the years was paying off, and in a very timely fashion—she now had 450 of them to direct in my absence.

In fact, Pathma was incredible. In the eye of the hurricane, she remained supremely in control. Somehow, in the midst of arranging my post-stroke care and coordinating my rehabilitation programme with the various health professionals, she also managed to run the company and handle the legal battle with our partners. Without her, I do not know how the company would have managed with me in such a weakened position.

The Battle Continues

Two weeks after the stroke, I received another unexpected visitor at the hospital. It was the spa owner, Nick Soh, who had put a wedge between my partner and me. Nick was concerned that my partner had stopped all transfers of inventory and staff from Body Contours to T Wellness. But my hands were tied, both by the legal dispute and by my physical state. (Note to readers: Nick Soh and T Wellness names are changed for privacy).

In childhood, I had been shown what a difference kindness could make in people's lives, starting with my own, and from then on, I became driven to continuously pay it forward. I truly wished to carry on with the business, but if it wasn't as clear to me before, it was crystal clear now that I would first need to help myself.

CHAPTER 4

FIRST STEPS ON A LONG ROAD

The journey of a thousand miles begins with one step.

–Lao Tzu[3]

Losing Myself

During this period, I felt tired all the time and could hardly stay awake. But the drowsiness was not the main concern. It felt as though I had become a different person.

From a competent communicator, I had suddenly, cruelly, become devoid of gestures and completely unable to articulate myself verbally. I had not just lost the ability to speak but also to process speech, so while I could hear conversations around me, they just sounded like babble. I could not understand a word that was being said. Yet, I had so much to express to those around me that I could only keep in my heart. Words completely failed me. Furthermore, due to the cognitive and communicative impairments, my attention span was greatly affected. It made me frustrated and anxious.

My temperament saw a stark change. Although this had arisen partly due to the fact that the stroke affected the part of my brain that regulated emotions, it was also a result of the overwhelming sense of powerlessness I felt.

I sometimes had little control over my own laughter and would laugh uncontrollably until I wept. Many people would have thought I was in a state of depression if they had seen that. But although having to deal with such a damaging disease may lead to depression, this is not always the case. I later read up on this, that there is an involuntary emotional expression disorder known as the *pseudobulbar affect* (PBA), which are sudden outbursts of emotion with no apparent cause. PBA may be brought on by neurological changes, such as with a stroke. When affected, a person may be prone to bouts of excessive laughter, crying, anger or sadness, although the outburst itself does not represent how the person actually feels at the time.

Rising from the Ashes

The stroke challenged every belief I had in myself.

I was Aanandha, the confident and capable individual who oversaw a large corporation, now reduced to grappling with the ordinary daily tasks that I previously never even had to think about. For the first time in my life, I felt utterly powerless. The unimaginable had happened and threatened to overwhelm me. Mundane things like speech and movement were now like foreign languages that had to be learned. I used to be so independent. Now I could not even use the toilet on my own! It was totally disorienting and not easy to accept this new reality. Was I ever going to be the same person again?

I struggled to remain hopeful. My loved ones fought on my behalf, doing what they could to lift my spirits and see to my rehabilitation. But their efforts could only go so far.

I had to fight for myself. I had to remember myself.

When my therapy first began, the team of health professionals took a few days to assess my situation and set things in motion. If there was one thing that they had all impressed upon me, it was this: My active participation in the therapy sessions was critical to my recovery. They guided me through the simplest of tasks patiently, taking great care that I did not completely lose my sense of self-esteem and dignity. No matter how many times I made a mistake, they would never get upset. They would simply guide me until I got it right. The sincerity I saw in their eyes greatly encouraged me.

Regaining Communication

Before my stroke, I hardly knew what a speech therapist was. I had assumed that my speech would return spontaneously to me—I mean, why wouldn't it? However, I had to consider that it would only return with hard work when, for the first 10 days, every time I attempted to speak my mind, all that came out was incoherent blabber.

Over the next weeks, I struggled to understand why my speech was the way it was. It was incredibly isolating, like being on an island on my own although surrounded by family, friends, and health care professionals. I could think, but I was still unable to verbalise whatever I wanted to say.

There were so many things I wanted to ask. I wanted to ask my wife how the company was doing. I wanted to ask how my mother and mother-in-law were, how my girls were. I wanted to know what had happened to me and how long it would take me to recover. Would it take a month? Longer? I did not realise at the time that recovery was going to be a very long and drawn-out process. And perhaps it was better that I hadn't been told.

Then, a spark of hope flickered. As we went through the twice-a-day therapy sessions, the first word tumbled from my mouth. 'Can!' I said. I was elated! My speech was slowly coming back, returning like drops of water from a tap, but still it was great news!

Through those sessions, I realised how remarkably complex the human machine is—just to make a sound, it involved having to consciously coordinate the movement of my articulators.

At first, I could recognise people but still not say their names. A few days after my first word, I managed to say 'can' a lot. I would reply 'can' to every request made of me and every question posed. Even though it was the only word I could say, for now, I felt that it helped me participate in a world that I had been abruptly ejected from.

My speech therapist, Hui Yong, tried to introduce a means by which I could say 'yes' and 'no'.

With much practice, I was able to use 'yes' and 'no' more reliably. However, I was still unable to tell people what I wanted—my mind was still in a fog.

Hui Yong set about introducing words she thought I would need for a basic level of interaction. We started with, for instance, 'water', 'thirsty', 'toilet', and 'towel'. I began to be able to use these words slowly.

Hui Yong, my speech Therapist

On 13 July 2012, a little more than a week after my stroke, I found out just how much effort learning to say 'good morning' from scratch really takes. Hui Yong had painstakingly taught me how to enunciate the word after a series of preliminary exercises with simple sounds like 'ah' and 'ee'. Initially, I was unable to move past the errors I made without guidance from the therapist, but I made progress to the point that I was able to self-correct those errors once I recognised them. Still, it would be a long while before I was able to spontaneously produce a sentence.

Going from day to day like this was a tremendous struggle. I had difficulty controlling the movement of my own tongue to produce even the most elementary sounds. What a living nightmare! I could not wake up from it. I felt powerless.

But, bearing in mind my health professionals' collective advice, I forced myself to use every single bit of my attention to participate and learn from the therapy. I would come away from a 30-minute session exhausted and just wanting to sleep, as though I had just completed an entire day's work at the office.

I wondered if Hui Yong ever felt exasperated with me. I really wanted to follow her instruction, but I had a hard time processing what she was saying. Furthermore, each motion that had been typically effortless before now required a painfully conscious effort on my part. My articulators, such as my lips and tongue, were not going to the right places despite my mind giving the instruction and despite Hui Yong's guidance. It seemed as though the right and left sides of my brain were not connected, preventing me from being able to follow simple directions.

For instance, I was able to count to 10 without any difficulty following Hui Yong's fingers, but I hesitated when asked to count the number of objects on the table. My daughter described an occasion when I had been asked to pick a toothbrush out of a line of items, but I had picked the hand towel instead.

When Hui Yong tried to teach me to say 'hello', no matter how hard I tried, my mouth would form the words 'good morning'. When she asked me to repeat 'apple juice', my mouth kept saying 'capple juice'. It was evident that I had to rebuild my entire vocabulary from scratch. I slowly learned to say words like 'papaya', 'banana', 'milo', 'mama', 'pa', although initially I could not associate the words with any image in my mind. I could just about mouth the words that were being said.

I also had to learn to identify parts of my body all over again, beginning with my eyes, mouth, and ears. At first, I was not able to point to them. It was only much later in my recovery, when Hui Yong explained the stages of the therapy, when I truly understood what had happened to me. At that time, it felt as though I was learning a completely new language with less than a three-year-old's vocabulary.

Nishta's motivational poster

In the midst of this waking nightmare, Hui Yong became a source of courage and motivation for recovery. It was in her patience and quiet confidence, the gentle way she worked with me.

There were many adjustments to be made by my speech therapist along the way. She had to consider not just my capabilities but also my personality. Before my stroke, and even as a young father to my daughters, I was someone who did not quite enjoy 'kiddy' activities. Of course, most of the therapy to practise my reading and comprehension skills employed material of a kindergarten level. Naturally, I did not enjoy the practice, and my family could sense that.

During one such session, my daughter recalled to Hui Yong that I used to enjoy reading the newspapers. Hui Yong immediately adapted passages from current affairs on Channel News Asia's website into the material.

Enjoying reading the newspaper

As the weeks passed, I came to understand the value of speech therapy and appreciate its benefits. I began to engage with my speech therapist, my friends, and family in a way that made more sense. It was a relief and a joy to be able to participate with the people around me again. I was no longer on an island and felt happy that the therapy was slowly able to draw me back into the circles of those who mattered to me.

There were those days when hope seemed completely lost. I felt the limits of having only half my body functioning. But then I would remember my wife and two children, and my will to fight would be renewed. I drew much consolation from the knowledge that I was not alone in my fight; I had my family, and they would do everything in their power to help me recover. I do not know what would have become of me without their support.

Meanwhile, the rate of improvement in my speech began to pick up over the next few weeks. I finally succeeded in stringing together full sentences, though not very coherently because I had to use many filler words. Nevertheless, all that time and effort was starting to pay off.

Regaining Balance

Before I started my physiotherapy sessions, I struggled to gain balance even when seated in bed—much like a baby. When I was propped up, I would slump down. My main physiotherapist, Siva, showed great enthusiasm. At times, he would wave excitedly at me saying that we shared the same name—Siva—which is also my first name. Had I been able to speak, I would have asked him to use my second name—Aanandha.

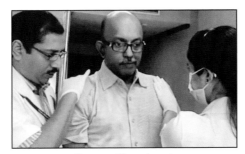

Siva, my Physiotherapist

He turned out to be very capable in handling me. He worked very well with my family and taught my wife, Pathma, many stretching exercises she could do for me, even while I was asleep. He stressed that it was important that I continue doing these exercises outside of our sessions.

In the early stages of my recovery, I had little strength in the right side of my body and was incapable of moving both my upper and lower limbs on that side. This meant that it was not possible for me to move my body without assistance.

He began each daily treatment with passive exercises and stretching. As I was bedridden, he needed to manually move my limbs to perform these motions. This ensured that my muscles maintained their flexibility and did not atrophy. I would watch him in bewilderment as he manoeuvred and stretched my legs for me, not understanding why I couldn't do this for myself.

The first movement I had to learn was how to turn so that I could go from a lying down position to a sitting position. My right muscles were weak, which meant I had to use my left hand to support my body.

This turned out to be an immense challenge. In the first few sessions, I could barely lift my body. Instead, my helpers had to move me. After a couple of sessions, I began to attempt to lift myself off the bed. Although this might seem insignificant, each milestone gave me a tremendous sense of achievement. I was happy that my nurses and allied health professionals were so capable in their work. I was in good hands. I then had to learn how to sit in an upright position. It was a strain to keep my body upright as I would often begin to slump down unless I had one person on each side to support my posture.

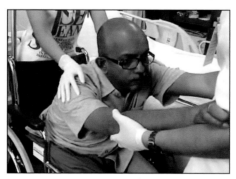

From sitting to standing position

The next milestone involved learning how to transfer myself from my hospital bed to the wheelchair. Being paralysed on the right side made me feel quite helpless, as I could not walk on my own. There was no sensation in my right leg; in fact, it did not feel like part of my body at all. I needed to get my right leg to function properly again, but I did not know how. Sometimes my brain had difficulty processing the instructions and remembering what to do; I could not follow Siva's steps. However, I did my best to do as he instructed and trusted in his expertise.

Once my muscles strengthened, and it was deemed safe enough, I learned how to move from a sitting position to a standing position. The physiotherapist's priority was to ensure that I got out of bed safely, as there was the risk of falling owing to my weak back muscles. Even when learning how to transfer myself from the bed to the sofa, I could not follow the instruction to lean my body forward to get balance since my trunk was not strong enough to lift my body.

Once I was able to stand upright, I was exposed to many weight-bearing exercises to regain further balance. As my right leg was significantly weaker than my left, these exercises forced me to put my weight on the weaker right side of my body, instead of making my left side overcompensate for my right side. This equal weight distribution was crucial to improving balance.

Again, as I lacked sensation on my right side, I relied completely on my therapist's instructions. This was not easy for me because I could not feel my right leg. It felt as though I was in an ocean, where the water was so deep my feet could not reach the ground. As I attempted to walk a few steps, my mind was like a whirlwind as I sought to balance my body. Although I was not comfortable doing this, my therapist continued to correct my every move-ment. At this stage of my recovery, one of the greatest challenges was having to keep my right knee straight, as it would always go into a bent position. Each time I attempted to put the weight on my right side, my right knee would bend. I was still relearning what it meant to put my weight on my right side. Because I could not balance, this made me unstable when I want-ed to stand up. My physiotherapist tried using a knee brace to keep my knee straight and force me to put my weight on my right side.

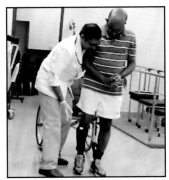

Braced for walking with Siva,
my Physiotherapist

In one of my therapy sessions, I needed two people, one on either side of me, and a walking stick to support my body as I sought to straighten my knee. As I moved my leg forward and back, they had to support my weight for me since my right leg was not strong enough.

Once I was able to stand up, I was exposed to many walking practices that helped strengthen my muscles and retrain my legs to walk, even without the sensory input from the right side. This lack of sensation made it more difficult to control my body. Apparently, the loss of sensation meant that I would not be immediately aware if I were to fall. I thought that these feelings of uncertainty in my movement were temporary, but they persisted for many years after the stroke.

As my movement improved, I progressed to using a quadripod—a walking stick with a stable base. When I first saw the contraption, my immediate thought was, 'This is for older people, not for a young man of 55!' However, this contraption was the only way I could hobble along with my therapist because it gave me support. I used my wheelchair most of the time because I could only walk using the quadripod for a maximum of 30 minutes. 'One fine day I will be able to walk again,' I kept telling myself. I pictured myself eventually being able to run 2.5 km like I used to. Running symbolised freedom to me because I used to jog to keep myself fit and, after the run, felt very energised and wonderfully de-stressed.

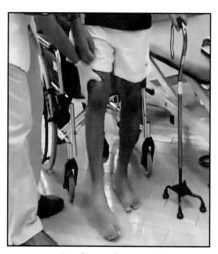

Quad – not for me at 55!

While my lower limbs were being worked on, both my physiotherapist and occupational therapist also ensured that I worked on my upper limbs. For instance, they worked on shoulder exercises with me as I was unable to lift my right hand on my own. I did assisted exercises for my right shoulder to move, which consisted of me using my left hand to grasp my affected right hand and lifting them together to do shoulder movements. I also did combined exercises for my shoulder and trunk to assist with my balance and kept working on my ability to move from a sitting position to a standing position. Again, my weight-shifting exercises while standing were important.

As I could not stand for long, I was often strapped to a table while doing my stand-and-reach and trunk exercises. That taught me how to shift and turn my body. Supported by the straps, I was able to stand without support from my therapist. I felt happy facing the window and looking out because it gave me a sense of liberation. The view consisted of a wide space between my building and the next one. I was a person who was always on the move, and this became one of my favourite spots in Mount Elizabeth. I literally felt my cares leave me as I looked far beyond.

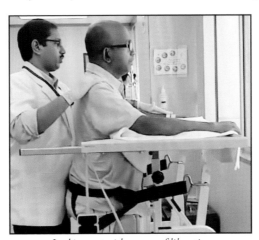

Looking out with a sense of liberation

Each day, the therapist would guide me through the passive shoulder exercises and shoulder movements. As my muscles were still very weak, the therapist was responsible for 90 percent of the movement, while I only contributed 10 percent. It was the same for my arm movements. When I did the stationary cycling, still from the wheelchair, it felt exhilarating as it reminded me of the days I used to cycle with my friends in 2002. When I was walking, I had a fear of falling, but I realised that Siva was extremely skilful and that there was no need to worry.

At first, the exercises were done in my room, but later, I could go in my wheelchair from the fifth to the eighth floor, to the rehabilitation room where the physiotherapist and assistant would need to slowly guide my walking—step by step. I could not understand why my right leg was still so immobile.

On my 55th birthday, I had to go home where my party was held. In order to be transported there, I needed a van with a special hoist to help me get into the van. I could not get into a normal car as my right leg was very stiff, and my back muscles were still weak.

On my 55th birthday

I must credit these daily exercises for my progress in movement and the quick improvement in the first six months to two years. Seeing my muscles being strengthened increased my confidence and spurred me on to persevere in my rehabilitation exercises. I was more intrinsically motivated to work on my walking because I saw the improvements more readily and also felt that the act of walking would give me a sense of independence quickly.

By September 2012, the last month I was warded in Mount Elizabeth, I was happy that I could walk with the assistance of a walking stick. I still needed Siva beside me because my right leg had difficulty holding my weight and this, in turn, affected my balance. My knee and ankle were not strong enough and could not be properly coordinated by my brain.

Siva started to get me to walk barefoot, which gave me the sense of being grounded. This was a lot harder because my sandals helped support my ankles and kept the toes aligned, whereas walking barefoot meant that my ankle had no external support, and my toes would tend to cramp together.

After I was discharged, I came to know about SpinoFlex, a kind of harness that hoists the trunk slightly off the ground so there is reduced risk of sustaining injury while trying to regain muscular function. As the harness supported my body weight, I had no fear of falling. I was also more willing to be challenged beyond what I would usually do, which meant greater stimulation of my brain. I later realised this to be the neuroplastic nature of the brain. For instance, I was willing to attempt heavier weight-bearing exercises and walk much faster than if I walked without this device.

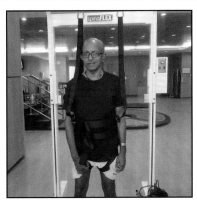

Spinoflex for balance with safety in 2013

While this was an encouraging development, my weak knee would sometimes buckle and my legs would hyperextend—that is, extend outward in a kind of kick. I also had issues with ankle stability that nearly caused me to sprain my ankle on many occasions. It took three years before I was able to walk with normal shoes. This was a significant achievement as it meant I did not require so much support for my ankle. Four years after my stroke, I continue to walk barefoot whenever I can. This means that my walking is coming close to normalcy, though it requires effort. But no longer does my right knee buckle or hyperextend.

It took me five and a half years to balance my body weight.

Regaining Flexibility

The stroke had caused my muscles to be extremely stiff. Physiotherapists refer to this as *hypertonia*, which is a common side effect of damage to the central nervous system after a stroke. It was difficult for me to stretch my limbs, which created severe loss of movement and sensation in my right arm and leg.

To assist with the overall physical rehabilitation, Pathma also arranged for InterX neurostimulation treatments. A therapist from Atos Wellness came to carry out the therapy every night for me. The InterX is a handheld device that delivers advanced interactive neurostimulation and is FDA approved for pain therapy. This device is commonly used by physiotherapists in the US and UK to assist with stroke recovery.

Pathma had asked Dr. Zulia if the InterX could be used as part of my stroke recovery. She confirmed that the InterX is commonly used for treating sports injuries and is used by the NFL, NBA, and many European rugby and football (soccer) teams. I received a 60-minute session every evening by a therapist on the protocol Dr. Zulia recommended for me.

Dawn, my occupational therapist, helped me improve my right arm's flexibility through many targeted repetitions. At first, we had two nurses to help me since my body was inflexible. The thought of attempting this feat alone seemed daunting. However, Dawn showed me a way to slowly move myself independently from the bed to the wheelchair and from the wheelchair to the therapist's couch in the physiotherapy room. Toward the end of my stay in Mount Elizabeth, Dawn taught me how I could even get into a taxi with minimal assistance.

Dawn, my Occupational Therapist

I now know that improvements in the arm take longer to develop than those in the leg. A stroke patient's upper limbs tend to take more time to recover than their lower limbs because the lower limbs have larger muscle groups compared to the upper limbs, making their function easier to regain. The fingers, too, require a higher level of dexterity to perform delicate tasks compared to the leg, so this muscle control takes longer to recover.

Dawn patiently continued to do weight-bearing exercises with me to regain the function of my hands. She suggested simple exercises such as shrugging, making small circular movements with the shoulders, and bracing, moving the shoulders backward and forward to ensure that the muscles were strengthened. In the early months, there were some signs that I had neglected my upper limbs as evidenced by my drooping shoulders. Thankfully, the physiotherapy was effective in preventing muscle spasticity.

Regaining My Fighting Spirit

My recovery was a team effort, right from day one.

Throughout this critical period, Pathma took it upon herself to listen attentively to the doctor's every word. She and our daughters took it upon themselves to ensure that I followed up on the activities from the therapy sessions. They would help me complete my speech therapy worksheets and practise the various physiotherapy exercises. Although I had previously been a highly motivated individual with a robust energy, the stroke now left me feeling extremely lethargic and groggy. I was thankful that my family continually prodded me to do my exercises, helping me push past my own limits and complete more exercises in a day. They also did what they could to ensure that I got sufficient rest between sessions.

Regaining My Humour

I had not seen the managers of my wellness centres for a few weeks at this point. These were people whom I used to see on a regular basis, men and women who had helped me build my business. Our reunion was a happy one.

I'm sure my appearance must have shocked them. But they tried to keep a brave front, even though some could not hold back their tears. I did not expect them to be that affected by my paralysis. I tried to cheer them up by saying—or at least trying to—that I would be better soon.

At that stage, I could only say a few words, and I was still mostly using the word 'can'. Realising this, my quick-witted managers soon jokingly asked, 'Mr. Aanandha, can we get a raise?'

'Can,' I replied, though I wanted to say no but couldn't. The best I could do was to shake my head at their mischief, as they laughed heartily.

How I had missed them!

Home at Last!

30 Sep 2012: I made my way home from Mount Elizabeth Hospital after three months. I was so glad to be finally back home. My home was made friendly for me—safe, accessible, and comfortable.

I looked forward to embarking on my rehabilitation journey to get back to work as soon as possible. Little did I realise that it would take more than nine years for me to be relatively independent.

It is still a journey that I will continue till I am fully independent of others.

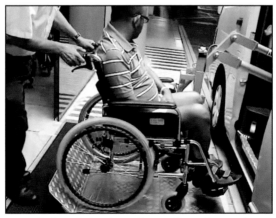

At the end of my hospital stay in September 2012

PART II: LIFE AS I KNEW IT

CHAPTER 5

MY BEGINNINGS

Every moment is a fresh beginning.

–T.S. Eliot[4]

My life began in 1957 in another hospital not too far away from where I was hospitalised after the stroke—Kandang Kerbau Hospital in Singapore, better known as KKH.

My Family photo in 1958 (From left, Sweeta my eldest sister with Papa; me with my Mama and Ron, my 2nd sister with Grandpapa)

I did not know it then, but I was born into a cusp of change.

At the time, Papa ran a thriving electrical business from his office at 11B Malacca Street with his uncle as partner. Malacca Street was the epicentre of change back then, with throngs of crowds and bustling markets and an immigration office down the street. Also the Singapore River was a major transport hub with ships moving in and out with fresh cargo. And there were none of those now-ubiquitous Western shopping malls in sight.

Fortuitously, his neighbour at 10A turned out to be none other than Lee Kuan Yew, with whom my father had studied at Raffles College in 1940. They parted ways when Lee Kuan Yew and his wife went to England. In 1959, Mr. Lee was on his own journey of change and independence, leading the country through an important transformation—Singapore's right to find its own identity independent of the British colonisers.

My father's classmate, Mr. Lee Kuan Yew, at Raffles College Alumni in 1993

But the tides of change continued to turn, and whatever curious circumstances had brought them together now saw them taking different paths. With the business, things went well for several years, until Papa, disagreeing on how the company should be run, made the bold move in 1960 to leave the partnership without compensation and search for a new beginning. I was three years old.

Papa never discussed his problems with Mama, but I could always tell from her anxious looks at certain times that the business was challenging

Papa's other classmate, Mdm Kwa Geok Choo

during those times. Then Papa made the decision to uproot the family, which now included four very young children, and move to Malaysia. The rest of the family was excited about the move because it would mean better opportunities for Papa and also a new set of friends, but I was torn up inside because it would mean leaving behind my beloved Uncle Guna. Guna was my father's younger brother, and he and my Aunty Olivia didn't have any children, so they treated me like their own son. I simply adored Uncle Guna because he was so much like my own papa. Both were kind and caring people who had a wonderful gift for reaching out to people in need and bringing out the best in everyone.

Papa now had his sights set on Kuala Lumpur. Taking the coast road, he drove to Port Dickson to inform close family and friends of our impending move to Malaya and to bring us to live temporarily at the government rest house. He knew we would be safe there under the watchful eyes of Uncle Selvarajah and Auntie Anne, and he then set off for Kuala Lumpur on his own in hopes of securing a tender for a lucrative electrical contract.

At our temporary new home, my siblings and I quickly grew restless. The lack of space, coupled with the unfamiliar environment, was a challenging combination for a mother with four children—the youngest of whom, Sri, was still in a cot. Fortunately, my uncle and aunt visited us the very next day and convinced Mama to move into their house where there was ample space and help with the children.

When Papa found out, he called Uncle Selvarajah to express his gratitude, but he also realised the pressing need to find a more permanent home for his family. Within days, Papa returned in his Ford Anglia sedan and relocated us to a small holiday bungalow close to the Selvarajah home. Since the facilities for cooking were not great, and there was insufficient kitchenware to prepare food, Uncle Selvarajah brought us our meals in tiffin carriers.

During those days, there were many lessons to be learned about patience and hard work. Mama did her best under the circumstances, but I was upset at being separated from Papa, and I missed him greatly. I ate little and sometimes suffered from a fever. Every day, I would wait for my Uncle Selvarajah to return home from work. I only ate food that was brought by my uncle, especially delighting in the fish broth. After dinner, I would crawl into his lap to listen to his stories and then fall asleep in contentment. Papa returned every few days to see us. Aside from Papa, Uncle Selvarajah and Uncle Guna were my role models at that age. They were men whom I wanted to emulate when I grew up.

Times were difficult, but we soon received good news. Papa had successfully secured the contract he desired, so we could finally live together as a family again! But although we were together, our troubles were not over, and I learned much from watching how my parents struggled. In his attempt to build his electrical business, Papa left the house early and returned late, and I rarely saw him. It was Papa who instilled in me the importance of hard work, and later in life, I made the same mistake as him by neglecting some of the important things in life.

With my father working late nights, my mother took care of the four of us. She had her hands full with cleaning, cooking, and attending to all our needs. Those days were difficult for her, I know; but for me, I fondly look back at that time.

The Selvarajahs and their early acts of kindness left an indelible impression on my parents and on me. Being so young, I may not have understood the full significance of what they did, but our family had found true friends in the Selvarajahs. They were there for us through our rocky adjustment period when we first moved to Malaya, and it was awhile before I began to understand the true impact of their small gestures of kindness at such a critical point in our lives. Uncle Guna, Uncle Selvarajah, and my father were very compassionate people who went out of their way to help others in need. I saw the difference that this made in our lives, and I decided at a young age that giving back to others was an example to follow.

They say that greatness begins with the little things. Growing up, I watched Papa run his business and lead by example. When I reached the age of 10, Papa began letting me follow him to work where I would run small errands for him. As I grew older, I became increasingly intrigued with the day-to-day operations involved in running a business. During my weekends and holidays, I would often go to the government hospitals with a friend to wash and apply sealant to the new floors to prevent them from absorbing stains. Sometimes I would assist Papa's workers, who also taught me a great deal. Also, my younger brother Sri and I would often accompany Papa on his long-distance contracts to Ipoh, Penang, and the eastern states.

I was so proud of Papa. He built the business from scratch, expanding it over 10 years. I keenly observed the way he treated his staff and formed relationships with them. He constantly asked them for feedback and would listen intently to their views. This helped them to build a great rapport with their boss. Although they respected him as their boss, they could still speak to him at any time about their personal problems, and they would find in him someone who was always willing to help.

My most memorable working experience with Papa occurred when I went to Singapore, at the age of 16, to demonstrate the use of concrete sealant to a tender team from the Port of Singapore Authority Warehouse. The sealant turned out to be exactly what they needed—durable, scratch-proof, and able to withstand oil and acids. With that, I got my first big order. I was so happy, and I glowed knowing that Papa was proud of me. From then on, Papa began delegating more jobs to me, and my confidence grew.

I attended the Methodist Primary School in Petaling Jaya for six years, finishing in 1969 when I was 12, and that was when Papa decided that his four children would become Malaysian citizens. I was school captain in my final year. Then I attended the Bukit Bintang Secondary School, graduating in 1974 with great results on my general certificate of education

O Levels—six A1s and one A2. Those scores landed me an Association of Southeast Nations scholarship from the Singapore government. It was a prestigious honour, and my parents were very proud.

Form 4 in 1973 Bukit Bintang Secondary School

With my parents' blessing, I moved to Singapore to pursue my scholarship in 1975 at National Junior College (NJC). It was there that I started challenging myself to achieve my academic goals, no matter how great the odds. The syllabus was heavy, and the pace of work relentless, but there was also something that I had not factored into my plans.

When I started school at NJC, I was already four months behind all my Singaporean peers because the Singaporeans got entry based on their preliminary O Level results (for examinations marked in Singapore), while the Malaysian students had to wait for their *actual* O Level results (for the official examinations marked in the United Kingdom).

With less than 18 months to prepare for the A Levels, I struggled to catch up, but despite my best efforts, my grades were mediocre: one B, two Cs, and a D. The contrast was stark next to the straight As I had scored just over two years before in my O Levels. It was a bitter disappointment. I was 19 and had just experienced what I saw as my first taste of failure. But the real question was, would I be able to pull myself back up?

I had one option left, and it was in India. I learned that I could study premed at a rural village outside New Delhi called Gurgaon. My plan was to serve humanity by working in a developing nation, but my grades were not good enough to enter the medical programme, so I redid my A Levels on my return home from India. I posted better grades in my second attempt, but it was still not enough. Perhaps I had underestimated the competition. Whatever the reason, I did not qualify. It looked like my dreams were being dashed.

Thankfully, Mama was there to catch me when I fell. With her help, I successfully applied to the Brunel University London to read medicinal and agricultural chemistry. It did not seem wise to delay my studies any further, but this required that I move once again, this time to a vastly foreign land. It wasn't easy for my parents to fund my studies, so I wanted to make sure that I did well.

During my years in the UK, I lived in relative solitude, but I learned how to live independently in a way that I might never have learned had I simply stayed in one place. Apart from my studies, I was chairman of the Overseas Student Association, which proved fulfilling and taught me the importance of organising activities for overseas students who were away from their families. I also spent six months each year working in the chemical industry as an intern at British Petroleum and the Ministry of Agriculture at Wye, a village in Kent.

Halfway through the course, I realised that a degree course in business might have been the more appropriate path. However, I did not want to change course, so I persevered and finished what I had started—a habit that Papa had taught me well.

These isolated student days were punctuated by a welcome visit from Auntie Selvarajah, who came on holiday. She immediately remarked on how confident I had become. I knew that I had changed, but I suppose it was more noticeable to her since we hadn't seen each other in a while. I was still Aanandha, but I had grown up. It was wonderful to see her again and to take her around the many places of interest, including Canterbury Cathedral, a vintage car display, and, of course, a famous fish-and-chips shop.

One evening in July 1980, I was reminded how far away I was from home. I was at a bus stop going about my own business when a bus pulled up and three skinheads got off. One of them walked straight up to me and, for no apparent reason, punched me in the face. Luckily for me, the skinheads simply went on their way, cursing under their breath. On the upside, the bus driver helped me up and offered me sympathy, thus quickly renewing my faith in people. That day, I understood that I would come across many different kinds of people and circumstances in life. I might not be able to control what was going on around me, but I could control myself, and that would help me prepare for the hard knocks that were still to come.

After four years in England, I graduated from the Brunel University London with second-class honours and prepared to return to the warm embrace of the sunny region I called home, full of reverence and excitement for the future. On the trip home to Malaysia, I thought of my mama, the anchor of my family when we were growing up. She cared for the kids while my papa was the sole breadwinner. Both of my parents ensured that all of us grew up to be independent, caring, and dependable people with compassion and integrity.

How different would life have been had I pursued my first dream of being a doctor in a developing nation? Papa didn't support me at first. And for me, it had become a struggle academically, and I'd lost my drive and direction for a while. Strangely enough, it didn't feel like a lost dream. I had found a new calling—going into business. Suddenly, I realised that I didn't have to be a doctor to serve humanity.

Leading with compassion and motivation were the tenets of people management that I learned from my early mentor, Uncle Guna, after watching how he was able to motivate his colleagues at the Central Provident Fund. They respected him so much that when he died in 1977, they took leave for half the day to show their final respects at his funeral. I wanted to build my business on the same set of beliefs.

CHAPTER 6

STARTING THE BUSINESS

So, what if, instead of thinking about your whole life, you just think about adding additional good things. One at a time. Just let your pile of good things grow.

–Rainbow Rowell[5]

The seed regarding going into business like my father was planted in my heart and mind on my return from the UK. My eyes sought a new frontier, and Singapore was an ideal place to start a business because of its infrastructure and support for start-ups.

The early years I had spent helping my papa in the business proved to be good preparation. He was my most influential mentor, and I learned from his successes and failures about what to look out for when doing business. That experience sharpened my business acumen and the way that I conducted myself as a businessman, so even though I was the head of a fledgling start-up when I set foot in Singapore, I was no novice.

My main business was selling carpet cleaning machines. Papa helped me get started by securing the Singapore distribution rights for the Rug Doctor machine from the United States. He even left some brand-new cleaning machines in Singapore, providing me with the inventory I needed to get going.

My Papa & Arul Selvam at an exhibition

What I needed next was a business partner, and I found one in Richard Ng, one of Papa's trusted contacts. Richard and Papa had successfully worked together before, and he seemed like a good fit, so we began operating from Richard's father's office on Stanley Street. The office was located on a busy street that sat on the west edge of Singapore's historical downtown core—the cultural epicentre. The 181-year-old Singapore Hokkien Huay Kuan building stood proudly just a few doors down and made us feel that the area was the place to build something that would withstand the test of time. It helped that we were able to get the unit rent-free, thanks to the generosity of Richard's father.

We were off to a great start, but we needed contacts. I had a few from Papa, but I still needed many more, so I set out every day from the YMCA on Palmer Road, where I stayed, armed with the giant Yellow Pages directory and a pocket full of change. I would find one of those boxy orange pay phones and make cold calls to carpet and contract cleaning companies, hoping I did a good enough job of masking the nervousness in my voice when asking whoever answered the phone for the opportunity to demonstrate the Rug Doctor at their office.

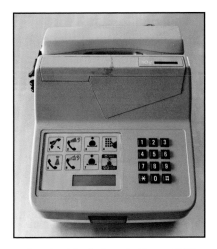

*I made cold calls from the Vintage 1971
boxy orange pay phone*

My first 'yes' came from Christopher and Sharon Tan, who ran Domic Carpet Cleaning on Upper Thompson Road. That first sales demonstration is etched in my memory forever. It began innocently enough with me showing them how to mix the cleaning solution with water and load it into the machine. Then I started the machine and dragged it across the carpet where the vacuum could work its magic. That's about as far as I got before I noticed that it wasn't just the carpet that was getting a shampoo but also my tie. I looked down and saw great blobs of foam coming out from the top of the machine. I'd been so flustered that I'd missed a step and completely forgotten to put the antifoam solution into the recovery tank. What a mistake!

I straightened up and tried to regain my composure as best I could with my tie dripping wet foam on the carpet. Thankfully, Sharon broke the silence when she burst out laughing, and her husband soon joined in. 'It's a good time to have a cup of coffee,' Sharon quipped, good-naturedly breaking the ice. That deal was closed over coffee, and more importantly, I had made some good friends.

That day, I learned something important: a company could only build a good reputation and a following if it had products and services that were both outstanding and reliable. Although I had messed up the demo, my machine spoke eloquently enough to sell itself. That's what it boiled down to. After 32 years later, the Rug Doctor continues to be a strong company in the United States, and Domic Carpet Cleaning still uses its machines to this day.

In 1984, Richard left the partnership to concentrate on his father's business, so I moved into my own office at Everton Park. It also became my home, which was exciting! I would work there during the day and sleep in a collapsible bed at night. Trying to build the business without a partner left me little time to socialise. My workday would start at eight thirty every morning and finish at nine o'clock every night.

Then I hired my first secretary, Rosalind Chow, to answer the phone and explain the machine to customers, while I did demonstrations at their offices and kept stock of our inventory. I enjoyed the challenge and the autonomy as the final decision-maker, but my work continued long after our office was closed for the day, and it wasn't long before that proved taxing.

We had done a good job of selling our machines, but we discovered that the machines that Atoz Enterprise sold needed maintenance, and we needed to provide access to that maintenance to keep our good name. Luckily, Arul Selvam stepped in at the right time because I would not have been able to grow my business without him. He was an engineer with Singapore International Airlines, and he arrived after work to help us. He was partly responsible for Atoz Enterprise's reputation for reliability, and that helped us expand our range of suppliers from the United States, Italy, and Germany. I was blessed to have the right people around me. As sales increased, I began expanding my range of products to include floor-cleaning machines (for washing floors) and also vacuum cleaners (for vacuuming floors and carpets). I didn't know many people in Singapore, so I made the effort to get to know my landlord, Mr. Yusof. I would drop by his office whenever I was in the area, and we would talk about the contract cleaning market. Mr. Yusof shared his contacts willingly, which I followed up on with his nephew, Abdullah Hameed. I could always count on him when I needed to transport my Rug Doctor machines for my office and showroom demonstrations.

My office at Upper Aljunied Road

Through Mr. Yusof, I also got to know Manjit Singh. Manjit ran his own company, which sold janitorial chemicals for maintenance, and we got on famously as a team. We were a great match—Manjit would supply the chemicals, and I would supply the machines—two complementary products that contract cleaners needed. As Manjit had been in the business for some time, it was easy to introduce my cleaning machines to his cus-

The Atoz Team

tomers. Manjit was also the person who introduced me to volunteer work, and he continues to be involved with me in many charities today.

Mr. Yusof, Manjit Singh, and Arul Selvam were my three earliest and closest friends whose support was a huge boost to my business. It was through them that I learned the importance of having trustworthy business associates. We still continue to share good times together to this day.

Sometime in 1984, a former classmate from NJC, Siany Bestari, introduced me to her husband, Adrian Chua, the area manager of Electrolux. Adrian's background was in marketing, while mine was in business development. A year later, he resigned from Electrolux to join me as a partner, and together, we started Atos Consumer Products Private Limited in Everton Park. Adrian and I decided to import Nilco vacuum cleaners (another of Papa's contacts from Germany). We hired a team of salespeople to do the direct sales and appointed Jansen Wong (formerly from Rainbow vacuum cleaners) as sales manager of the team who sold them door-to-door.

Teatime after sales meeting

The work was challenging, but we kept our team spirit strong by re-grouping at teatime over coffee and toast. If our sales meetings extended past 10:00 p.m., we would share a supper of *ikan Pari* (a kind of spicy stingray dish) and *roti prata* (a southern Indian pancake made of stretched dough and served hot off the griddle) while discussing the day's activities.

I always looked forward to the weekends when I would return to Malaysia to be with my family. Papa continued to be an adviser, coach, and mentor to me, while his wisdom and work ethic remained a constant inspiration. Like him, I didn't ever want to retire. I had reached a point where I was thankful for the many challenges that arose and the unexpected opportunities that surfaced from them.

My advisor, coach & mentor

But I was soon faced with another challenge when increasing competition in the vacuum cleaner business inspired me to diversify into the beauty and wellness business. But before that could happen, someone even more unexpected and unfamiliar came into my life. Her name was Pathma.

CHAPTER 7

STARTING A FAMILY

Families are the compass that guides us. They are the inspiration to reach great heights and our comfort when we occasionally falter.

–Brad Henry[6]

'Aanandha, I want you to meet a young lady who will be a very suitable match for you.'

That's what my Uncle Vasagar said when he called me one day in August 1990, and a meeting was quickly arranged. In true Ceylonese tradition, Pathma was accompanied by her mother, eldest sister, and brother-in-law, and I learned that she was the head of English at a secondary school.

The chemistry was there right away, and I felt happy seeing the spontaneous way she would smile and laugh. It was love at first sight! That young teacher immediately won my heart with her freshness and her air of innocence. Somehow, I sensed that she would be my wife.

We started to meet after work, and I looked forward to every one of those evenings during the months of our courtship. In March 1991, we were married, and we moved into our own apartment.

Our first daughter, Nishta, was born in 1993, and our second daughter, Triynka, was born soon after in 1994. The two girls got on well, playing with their dolls together and watching *Barney & Friends* on television. I thank God to have been blessed with a wife like Pathma. She could always be counted on to see to the needs of the home and family, including tutoring the children in their studies. Even though she had many responsibilities in her teaching profession, she gave herself to the family wholeheartedly and without complaint.

Mr. & Mrs. Ananda Rajah

One day in 1998, while I was having a sales meeting at my office, I received a call from Pathma, and I could immediately sense the panic in her voice. Nishta, then only five years of age, had fallen from the playground slide and hit her head on the ground. Her teacher was worried because Nishta was vomiting. It didn't look good. I rushed to the kindergarten with Pathma, and we took Nishta to the hospital. A brain scan revealed a small fracture in her skull, and Nishta was scheduled for an operation the very next day. My wife and I spent the night in the hospital. As we prayed for God to heal Nishta, my anxiety lifted, and I firmly believed that God was in control of the situation.

The following day, for some reason, the surgeon decided to perform another scan. He was dumbfounded to discover that the fracture was no longer there! It was nothing short of a miracle. It felt as though our prayers had been answered in our time of need.

Nishta & Triynka Ananda

Looking back on it now, I wish I had accompanied my children to the playground more often, instead of working as hard as I did. Not that I could have prevented her accident, but my greatest regret is working so much that I couldn't spend more time with my young family.

CHAPTER 8

STARTING IN WELLNESS

Wellness is the complete integration of body, mind, and spirit—the realization that everything we do, think, feel, and believe has an effect on our state of well-being.

–Greg Anderson[7]

It was becoming more apparent by the day that there was greater potential in the wellness market than in the market for industrial machines. Armed with a growing interest in wellness products, I attended an exhibition that displayed beauty machines from all over the world. Soon after, our company began importing two products for beauty salons—the Bioptron lamp from Switzerland in 1991 and Proslim equipment from the UK in 1992.

I was amazed by both of these pieces of equipment that provided beauty solutions not otherwise attainable at that time. The Bioptron lamp was used to improve facial conditions such as acne, wrinkles, and pigmentation, while the Proslim equipment was used to tone the body through passive exercise. It involved placing pads over the muscles to deliver a mild electrical current that caused contractions similar to those one would experience through physical exercise.

We sold 90 Bioptron lamps and 100 Proslim machines between 1991 and 1994, but after three years of selling wellness equipment, our sales to beauty salons began to plateau, and the harsh reality was that I now had to look for more business opportunities. My decision to move directly into the consumer market for slimming and beauty was a natural progression that came with a number of challenges.

Then we made a strategic decision. We set out to penetrate the beauty and wellness industry by setting up our own beauty and wellness centre. That would allow us to tap into the rapidly growing wellness market, which would hopefully prove more lucrative than our existing business model of selling equipment. With the industry growing, we could provide excellent products and services directly to the customer while drawing in a much larger repeat clientele. Many companies were already targeting their products and services at this market, and the statistics showed a rising demand for beauty and wellness services, especially among women aged 30 to 55.

More than that, I had ambitions of expanding the company internationally. That desire came from watching my father grow his company over the years. Empowered by my father to accept responsibility from a very young age, I had grown up with the desire to empower others. That formed the basis of my management style in Atos. It gave our employees plenty of space to grow, which, in turn, accelerated our overall productivity.

Credit must go to my father for sharing with me the value of running a business ethically and developing human capital. As a result, the rapport he built with his employees paid off many times over. Those priceless insights became part of my blueprint for how to build a successful business. They included the importance of building strong teams and always being attentive to the staff—listening to their concerns or suggestions.

In 1995, we opened our first Atos Wellness centre, under the brand Slimline Studio, in Far East Plaza in Singapore. We provided massages, facials and body contouring. The rental for the 500-square foot office was high, but the prospects were thrilling. We had just started a new business, and we had the right team. We opened our first centre with only four trained therapists, but they all held professional beauty certifications, and they also received specialised training on the equipment from our UK suppliers, Sue and Sandy Marshall from Slim Images. That foundation enabled them to integrate their existing knowledge with specialised overseas training to meet and exceed the expectations of our clients. And Malkit

Kaur, who had joined me four years earlier as the chief demonstrator when we were selling to beauty salons, stepped up to become the manager of our flagship beauty salon.

Slim Images Principals – Sandy & Sue Marshall 1992

Although the first year was exciting, we soon ran into our initial round of challenges. It proved difficult to recruit employees who were willing to work until 9:30 p.m. That was an essential requirement as our clients usually came for their sessions after office hours. Since we lacked a customer base, we could only afford small advertisements with our limited funds. Our first advertisement in the *Straits Times* cost $2,000, and it invited readers to fax a coupon in for a free trial. To my delight, 30 people responded, which was beyond my expectations since the advertisement had only been intended as a trial run. We gave all of these customers the best service we could possibly provide. In the meantime, the response to our advertisements continued to pick up.

Within six months of starting the first centre, I realised that one centre was not enough, so in 1996 we rented another 800-square-foot shop in the Adelphi, where we opened the second Atos Wellness centre under the brand name Slimcare Studio.

During the first year of operation, cash flow became a major problem. Investments from family and friends were vital, as no banks were willing to risk lending such a large sum of money to a small start-up business with no track record. I was thankful for the strong, supportive role of my friends, and also Pathma's family, during our time of need.

With hard work, we were able to keep the business profitable, and once those profits were sustainable, we then expanded our vision. In 1997, Manjit Singh introduced me to Michael Goh, who was looking for a new business opportunity. With Michael's investment, we launched Body Contours, and our first outlet was located in Katong Mall. Business was so good that we soon did not have enough treatment rooms to accommodate our clients, which prompted us to consider opening new centres.

Both Atos Wellness (then Slimline and Slimcare) and Body Contours were thriving. Since Body Contours focused on weight loss and facials, we decided, in 1998, to create another brand, Body Wellness, that focused on spa and wellness. We sent our trainers to an exhibition in Milan, where they were exposed to the latest innovations in the beauty industry. Among the many brands displayed, O'Derme and Natura Bissé stood out, and we signed the distribution rights for both of the brands. Training in Italy and Spain followed, and it quickly paid off when it enabled our staff to gain a deeper knowledge of the skincare industry and become more adept in using the latest technology.

Business took off! And we expanded through recommendations and referrals. Having separate brands that offered distinctly different products and services allowed us to reach out to a wider range of customers without diluting each brand. That formula worked well for us. We continued to invest in high-tech machines in the beauty and wellness market, and our clients were getting excellent results.

At first, I was responsible for running Body Contours while Michael took care of Body Wellness. In 2001, Michael and I decided to do a share swap, with him taking Body Wellness and me taking Body Contours. It was around that time when Pathma joined me in the business as an understudy to help Atos Wellness improve its operational efficiency and staff training.

I engaged Gerald Lim, a business development manager, to market Atos Wellness to the corporate world, and as our marketing team grew, we formed a telemarketing team. Seeing that Gerald needed space to grow, I proposed we create another company, and we started Subtle Senses in a shophouse on Mosque Street. It did very well, but Gerald and I disagreed on the growth plans. In 2005, the company no longer required my involvement, so we decided to go our separate ways, and I asked Gerald if he would buy my half of the company. I embarked on Inner Harmony, which was positioned as an upmarket wellness centre, while Gerald continued to excel in the business as CEO and owner of Subtle Senses. In 2009, he became the youngest Singaporean to win the Rotary-ASME Entrepreneur of the Year award, while I received the Spirit of Enterprise award.

"I believe when we help others, we will be helped in return."

Spirit of Enterprise, 2009

CHAPTER 9

EXPANDING INTO A NEW FRONTIER

It is impossible to live life without failing at something unless you live so cautiously that you might as well not have lived at all.

–J. K. Rowling[8]

Teaming Up with Medec

Both Atos Wellness and Body Contours were becoming more established, so many possibilities lay ahead of us, including the chance to fulfil my ambitions of expanding the brand overseas. To achieve that, we could either merge with similar companies, or better yet, merge with similar companies with public listings. I did not have to wait long for an opportunity to present itself.

Back in 2003, I had met Josef Plattner who was the CEO of Medec Limited, an Australian-listed company that sold wellness products. We purchased 10 Bioresonance mats for trials in Singapore, and Josef and I would meet whenever he was in town. Two years later, he mentioned that he was looking for a business to acquire, and I asked if he would consider Body Contours. With a strong corporate team and a diverse board of directors, the company's growth would most certainly be accelerated to an exciting new level. The acquisition would also facilitate the expansion of Body Contours into Australia.

In April 2006, I went ahead with the plan for Medec to acquire 51 percent of Body Contours, and I flew to Perth to meet the Australian directors. They were suitably impressed by what they were shown, and we signed a head of agreement. After three months of due diligence, the acquisition was complete, and Medec became the major shareholder of Body Contours. Before the acquisition, I owned 75 percent of Body Contours. By selling 51 percent, I received $625,000 and 4.5 million Medec shares.

As forecasted, Body Contours's performance did better in 2007 and 2008, in part due to having an international board of directors, which included two Australian directors and two from Singapore. That was my main reason for selling our majority stake in Body Contours to Medec. I believed that our listing as a public company was key to positioning Body Contours for expansion into Australia and beyond. We were now set to make our move into other countries, such as India and Malaysia, in addition to our base in Singapore.

About nine months after Body Contour's acquisition, one of the major shareholders of Medec called an emergency general meeting, citing Medec's underperformance in many of its subsidiaries. Much to our shock, CEO Josef Plattner stepped down because he felt that his best was not good enough for the company shareholders. Since there was no one to replace him as CEO of Medec, Josef asked me if I would allow my company, Atos Wellness, to become a part of Medec. It was an attractive proposition that could increase Medec's annual turnover. Atos Wellness's performance over the past 23 years would boost shareholder confidence, so a reverse merger of Atos into Medec was proposed, which meant that Medec Limited would be renamed Atos Wellness Limited with me as the CEO of the public company. In this reverse merger, Pathma and I would receive only Medec shares, which meant that we would own 60 percent of the public company. This was possible because Medec did an independent expert's report that showed that this reverse merger would benefit Medec shareholders. An extraordinary general meeting was held whereby Medec shareholders agreed to the reverse merger.

Atos went public for the same reason as Body Contours: to raise capital for our global expansion plans. In an effort to consolidate our activities,

I had previously assisted in the divestment of the nonperforming Medec subsidiaries, including Athlegen, Inspired life, and Bodycure, that were not directly related to the spa and wellness industry. By January 2008, Atos Wellness did a reverse merger with Medec Limited so Atos Wellness Limited was formed. I could hardly believe that I was the CEO of a company that was listed in the Australian and German exchanges. I was not paid a salary, but I received options if the company did well. With international branding, we were set to go places. That called for champagne!

Success Permissions

In 2009, I attended a course that centred on transactional analysis. It was by Dr. Sundardas Annamalay, whom I had known since 1990. I attended this course together with my key staff and saw that it helped increase the turnover of our companies by a significant amount. I realised that this course was able to clear subconscious blocks for my team and me. Our sales in Body Contours went up from $1 million to $2 million a month in a matter of six months. Transactional analysis holds the secret to business success. Understanding the impact of transaction analysis is critical to managing your people and thus business success. Up to then, I had tried to improve the performance of my company significantly but could not achieve this until I attended that course.

But trouble was brewing. While I was running the public company between 2008 and 2010, a major unforeseen issue began to emerge. Within four months of the reverse merger of Atos Wellness Limited, the global financial crisis crippled the global economy, and it suddenly became more difficult to raise capital. To make up for it, we had to dig into the company reserves, which we had set aside for our expansion plans into Chennai, Kuala Lumpur, and Vienna.

It was becoming painfully clear that we lacked the necessary human resources and infrastructure to run the new Asian and European centres. We didn't have all the franchise documentation to properly conduct our overseas operations, so we had to stop operating in Perth, Chennai, and Kuala Lumpur. It was a painful reminder that success in Singapore did not automatically translate into success elsewhere.

So, for Atos Wellness Limited, we had to rethink our expansion plans and consolidate our business in Singapore.

Changes Ahead for Atos Wellness Limited

In the wake of the global financial crisis, Singapore's spa and wellness industry took another hit. Consumer confidence reached at an all-time low in this uncertain climate. Elsewhere in the industry, there was news of spa closures including Wellness Village, Simply Spa, and Wax in the City, to name just a few. This dampened the growth fever in the spa and wellness industry and began to cause consumer fear regarding prepaid packages. Therefore, there was a need to unify the spas so we could gain back the waning confidence in our wellness industry.

In December 2009, Atos Wellness Private Limited had succeeded in coming to the aid of a faltering company, Wellness Village. This time, we initiated the move to rally a group of spas. Together, we made a public show of solidarity by offering to take in Simply Spa and Wax in the City customers. Such goodwill was unprecedented, and it was intended to restore the trustworthiness of the spa industry in the public eye. The local papers caught on, and we made the news.

In 2010, when True Spa faced difficulties and approached me, I once again garnered the support of 20 spas so that all True Spa's customers were covered. Between 2009 and 2011, our various 'spa-rescue' initiatives took in more than 10,000 clients of distressed spas. These moves highlight an important principle: There is a time to compete, and there is a time to unite and work together for a broader goal. The broader goal in those uncertain times was ensuring continued consumer confidence in our industry.

In this climate, people were hesitant to sign up for high value packages, which affected the performance of Atos Wellness Limited. So, it came as no surprise when, in the middle of 2010, the Australian directors of Atos Wellness Limited requested that I buy out the shares in the companies that I had originally owned: Body Contours, Atos Wellness, and Inner Harmony. This was a great blow to my dreams of expansion. However, considering market realities, I had to admit that this was the most practical thing for me to do. I did not have the funds to buy back all three companies in one go, so I proposed that I buy them back in stages: first Body Contours and then find an investor to help buy back Atos Wellness and Inner Harmony. The Australian directors were agreeable to this.

I began my search for an investor to buy out my three companies, but I had no idea where the trail would lead. What I didn't realise was that things were moving behind the scenes at a breakneck pace. What happened next was a series of events I could never have imagined. First, in the third quarter of 2010, a friend provided a loan that allowed me to buy out the 51 percent share of Body Contours owned by the public company. Now, the heat was on to find an investor to repay him.

A New Partnership: The Mayar Group

Next, the Mayar Group from India stepped forward with an expression of interest. I had been introduced to one of its directors a year earlier by a good friend. Similar to how my father had started his business, Mayar also had humble beginnings during India's early independent days. Their founding visionary tapped into India's paper trade, and they later expanded to become a global conglomerate over a span of decades. Among its core businesses was its upmarket wellness company headquartered in New Delhi. It became clear to me that with a presence across five continents and six key industries under its umbrella, including infrastructure, oil, and drilling, the Mayar Group was a giant—and they were showing a keen interest in us. I had first met Abhit Sud, the son of the founder of Mayar, in New Delhi in 2010. I was with Pathma and my mother, and we had dinner with his family in New Delhi. We got along well, and I was happy that Mayar would eventually own 50 percent of our three companies.

We entered into discussions, and after a due diligence, the Mayar Group decided to buy 50 percent of Body Contours; and they agreed to buy 50 percent of Atos Wellness and Inner Harmony when they left the public company in Australia. We formed Atos-Mayar in December 2010. Body Contours came in first, and Atos Wellness and Inner Harmony joined the group in July 2011. I was appointed CEO. This was the beginning of my partnership with the Mayar Group. Little did I know that our partnership would soon be put to the ultimate test, but for the time being, the assurance of continued success seemed almost set in stone.

Once the Australian directors had divested themselves of the three Singapore companies, they still needed a new business for Atos Wellness Limited (the Australian holding company of which I was still the CEO). In 2013—by which point I had resigned as CEO because of my stroke—they found it in Fitgenes, a company devoted to a genetics-based approach to health. The name Atos Wellness Limited was changed to Fitgenes Limited.

CHAPTER 10

THE BREAKUP

It is the unexpected that changes our lives.

—Unknown

Yet Another Spa in Distress

However, our troubles were far from over. As a backdrop to our success in finding a strong partner, the spa situation continued to deteriorate.

In August 2011, we received another cry for help from Nick Soh, the owner of T Wellness. I had been introduced to Nick more than 10 years before when we each volunteered at the St Joseph Home. Nick and I went way back, and I considered him a good friend, so I didn't hesitate to leap to his rescue when he was in trouble. I was confident that we could duplicate our past successes, but things were to play out very differently this time around. The chain of decisions that followed created an unstoppable domino effect with consequences that reached far into the future for everybody, especially for me; but on the surface, everything was deceptively calm.

In August 2011, Body Contours stepped forward to commit resources to assist T Wellness's needs for wellness products so they could continue their operations. We also needed another $200,000 in capital, but I was confident that the other spa owners would team up to help me bail this spa out. However, I was told by three other owners that they lacked the time and resources to contribute. Still, I was determined to achieve what I had set out to accomplish. It was a matter of principle.

I approached my friend Tan Bien Kiat, the managing director of Titan Capital, and he agreed to invest $100,000 in the rescue package for the spa, but he had one condition—Body Contours had to invest an equal amount of capital in good faith. Since we were jointly owned by the Mayar Group, the investment needed their consent.

Unfortunately, this was nowhere near the end of the saga. It soon became clear that rescuing T Wellness would involve more than finance. Body Contours had to send four veteran staff members to help the ailing spa win back clients. It was touch and go for a while, but the plan worked, and in the third quarter of 2011, T Wellness's performance started to pick up. It looked like we were in the clear, but nothing is ever that easy.

The Breakup

During our initial conversation with T Wellness, we had agreed that for Body Contours's investment on inventory, we would have the option to exercise the right to own 50 percent of the spa—providing, of course, that the spa recovered. At this time, Body Contours itself was still buried in the transition of integrating Aura Day Spa (an Atos-Mayar spa project) into its operations. The transfer of our key staff members only added to that burden. Nonetheless, I was confident that Body Contours would stay on top of things because we had very experienced and reliable staff to help lead us through this rough patch. However, having to pump inventory into the struggling spa did not sit well with my Mayar partners, who owned the other half of Body Contours. They were less optimistic than I was about the survival of T Wellness, and they were concerned that we might be pouring money down the drain to revive a company that was on the way down.

Abhit felt that our resources were already stretched, but I saw the long-term benefits for Atos-Mayar, and for the spa industry in general, if we could transition the turnaround of the spa. There was no denying that there were sacrifices that had to be made in terms of staff and inventory, but I felt that it was a good strategic move and that the timing was right.

T Wellness had a stable customer base and only required cash flow and a capable management team to turn it around, so my calculated goal of ultimately acquiring 50 percent of the spa would be a win-win situation for both T Wellness and Body Contours. I spoke of Titan Capital's willingness to invest $100,000 in the spa to help make my case to Abhit and then arranged for him to meet with Tan Bien Kiat in September 2011.

Surely Abhit would agree that the matching $100,000 investment should come from Body Contours and not me personally. Nick Soh wanted to go to Australia, and the plan was that T Wellness would eventually be owned by Body Contours and Titan Capital. However, despite all my efforts to persuade Abhit, he refused to budge. I tried to assure him that this investment was our stake in the spa and that it was only a matter of time before the spa would be taken over by Body Contours and become part of the Atos-Mayar Group. However, by the first quarter of 2012, The Mayar Group remained unsupportive.

As a last-ditch effort, I gave Abhit my personal guarantee that I would see to it that the company was reimbursed if Body Contours was disadvantaged in any way. However, the mounting outflow of inventory from Body Contours to T Wellness had already amounted to $700,000 over the past months, and this did not sit well with him.

In March 2012, I received a call from Abhit Sud that was unlike any other conversation we'd had up to that point. I listened carefully as he expressed his grave concern over my continued support of T Wellness. He felt that we had put Body Contours at great risk, and as chairman of Atos-Mayar, he delivered the group's verdict that I was not living up to their expectations of a CEO. My heart sank.

There was a brief pause on the phone. 'This is our final decision,' he said. 'I'm sorry, Aanandha.'

I said nothing. Although disappointed that we could not see eye to eye on such a crucial matter, I had to accept that we had reached an impasse. There was no more room for negotiation. After the call, I braced myself for the worst possible scenario and that soon occurred when I received a registered letter at the office in a nondescript sealed envelope. I opened it and skimmed through the documents. The heavy grain of the paper felt like a stone in my hand. It was a lawsuit filed by the Mayar Group.

Wanting to preserve the relationship and avoid any form of litigation at all costs, I repeatedly assured Abhit of how much Body Contours would eventually benefit by the acquisition of T Wellness and that all we had to do was support it over the short term. But he did not share my vision of a positive outcome. His mind was made up. He had lost all confidence in me, and he was going to pull out.

As the deadline neared, there was no escape hatch to be found. The walls were closing in on me fast. Try as we did, we were unable to raise the funds in that limited time. We reached out for help, but our company and the years of hard work were buried by the sand in the hourglass. Then came 30 June 2012. Checkmate.

Little did I know that a more serious and debilitating fate awaited me only days later. On 3 July 2012, I had my stroke.

Seeking Closure

The legal tussle continued during my recovery. In March 2013, I decided to pick up the phone to call Abhit Sud. That was the last thing my family wanted me to do. They didn't want me to do anything that would take my focus off trying to heal my body, but I was anxious to settle the matter.

The phone rang a few times, and I thought it was going to go to voice-mail when a familiar voice on the other end answered, 'Hello, Aanandha,' and then after a brief pause, he continued. 'What can I do for you?'

My muscles struggled to move and enunciate my words. 'I would like for us not to fight,' I said as steadily as possible. The legal fees were mounting, and it was costing both of us a literal fortune. Settling out of court seemed like the more sensible and sustainable solution, and our own lawyers had advised us to do just that.

My partner pondered the olive branch carefully. 'Yes, I would like to put an end to it as well.' If he was feeling relieved, there was no indication of it in his voice. However, by the end of the conversation, we agreed to amicably part ways. Mayar became the 100 percent owner of Body Contours while Pathma and I acquired 100 percent of Atos Wellness and Inner

Harmony. Nevertheless, I was left with a flat, empty feeling in my heart. I deeply regretted the breakup.

Post-Breakup

When news of the breakup with Mayar got around, Nick Soh, owner of T Wellness, dropped in to see me at my home and asked for my help. He had previously visited me at the hospital, but I was unable to respond properly. Now that Atos was independent again, and I had gained some measure of my functions, I assured Nick of my continued support. Atos Wellness was now fully responsible for the $700,000 inventory that had originally been committed to T Wellness on the tacit understanding that it would eventually own 50 percent of the spa.

Inventory continued to flow to T Wellness and business improved. That did not come as a surprise, as I had calculated the odds from the beginning. I was excited for the next challenge, and I saw so much potential as we were in the process of rising from the ashes together. There were even more ways that I could help T Wellness. They had an outlet on Orchard Road, and its monthly rent was more than $100,000 per month. When the lease came up for renewal, I took the opportunity to negotiate a lower rate with the landlords and got them to reduce the price to $60,000 a month, which would immediately save T Wellness $500,000 a year in overhead.

All was going well until I got an unexpected visit from Christina Lau, who had been brought in to work at T Wellness while I was in recovery. 'I think there's something you should be aware of,' she said, visibly upset.

It turned out that during one of her discussions with Nick, he claimed to be the sole owner, which was untrue. We had already come to a verbal understanding that we had the option of taking over 50 percent of T Wellness any time we wanted to, but now that the spa was doing well, it seemed that this option was going to be put aside by Nick.

In December 2013, Nick stopped responding to my calls and emails. It was then that I realised he had decided to maintain full ownership. All he intended to do was to repay the capital investment of $200,000, and the $700,000 worth of inventory we had contributed. Nick was able to do that because we didn't have a written agreement in place. I had known him for more than 10 years and considered him a close friend who was in dire need of help at a critical time. So, I didn't think a written agreement was necessary, but I was wrong.

I felt utterly betrayed, and I was too numb to speak. Our involvement in T Wellness had come at great cost—both on the corporate and personal front. Apart from all the resources that had been pumped into the business, the greatest damage I sustained was the falling out with my friend and business partner, Abhit Sud. Had I not staked so much to help Nick and T Wellness, my relationship with Abhit would not have been fractured. More importantly, I might have avoided a highly stressful financial and personal crisis that contributed to my stroke.

When later asked why I had wanted to help Nick, I gave the same reason that I always did. 'If that spa had gone under, many customers would have been stranded and the entire industry would have suffered.'

I learned the difficult and cruel lesson that *all* agreements needed to be put in writing for *everyone's* protection. What did that mean for my own principles and my faith in the goodness of people? Would this experience leave me bitter and less trusting of everyone? They say that one must learn how to forgive and let go, but no matter how I tried, the memories haunted me. I had to learn how to free my mind.

PART III: TRANSFORMED INTO A STROKE OF GRATITUDE

CHAPTER 11

THE PLAN YOU WISH YOU DIDN'T NEED

Before anything else, preparation is the key to success.
–Alexander Graham Bell[9]

Waking up in my own home felt like a blessing. But as I drew in a deep breath and closed my eyes, the same futile thoughts ran through my mind. *Where did I go wrong? What could I have done differently? What shouldn't I have done? What if…? If only…*

The truth was that things could have been a lot worse. I had dropped down into an abyss with no end in sight, only to be caught up in a cocoon-like safety net. It was a narrow escape. Luckily, a little sprinkle of foresight here and a pinch of planning there had helped me develop that safety net, despite my misplaced trust in the spa owner.

One of our greatest fears is of being hospitalised, and I was no exception. It's not because we fear death but because we fear that sickness will lead to a permanent loss of our familiar lifestyle. We also fear getting a hospital bill that could potentially curtail our freedom to enjoy life as we had planned. In the field of medicine, Singapore easily stands shoulder to shoulder with the best of the best. During my three months in the hospital, I received the finest care possible. Then, when the hospital bill arrived, I didn't have to worry about a thing since I had been prepared—but that was by chance.

I had always agreed with the theoretical importance of having insurance to cover me in the event of an illness, but I remained reluctant to invest in a medical and critical illness term insurance policy because I felt that I was healthy and would not need it. When agents approached me, my usual excuse was that I was too busy with work to meet them. But in 2011, Ashvin Das asked me to give him an hour of my time to discuss my existing policies. I don't know why I said yes; maybe it was just good timing on his part. When we got down to having the chat, it didn't take long for Ashvin to find out that I was not covered by any medical insurance or critical illness policy whatsoever. I hadn't intended to purchase a plan with him, but he told me a story that made me reconsider.

One of his clients had assumed he was healthy and did not need medical insurance. In the end, he decided to purchase a plan, and he wound up being extremely grateful when he needed that plan at a critical time in his life.

I discovered that it only required a small monthly investment. I was surprised that the insurance was affordable and that the coverage was more extensive than I had envisioned. It would include hospital stays, potential rehabilitation, and outpatient costs. Furthermore, I would enjoy lifetime coverage with a limit of $500,000 a year if I needed it.

So, after a rather lengthy discussion, he finally convinced me to invest $440 a month for a policy that would have me fully covered. Because I had taken the time to listen to Ashvin and then decided to put aside $440 a month, my entire bill for hospitalisation and outpatient care was covered. Without that policy, that bill would have caused me a great deal of stress. Instead, it allowed me the freedom to focus on my recovery.

There is no doubt that peace of mind helped me in my recovery. I was so fortunate that my insurance plan allowed me to recover in a hospital. Also, it meant being able to afford more sessions with the physiotherapist, occupational therapist, and speech therapist, all of whom were instrumental in my rehabilitation. Had I not purchased insurance when I did in 2011, I would have been uninsurable after the stroke.

Almost immediately after I suffered the stroke, Ashvin came to assist me and my family with my medical claims. It immediately became clear that having the right insurance agent is very important. Thankfully, Ashvin had initiative, which he demonstrated at this critical time in my life.

CHAPTER 12

RECOVERY IS NOT A STRAIGHT LINE

Life is not a problem to be solved, but a reality to be experienced.
—Soren Kierkegaard[10]

I was told that sometime between three and six months after my stroke, the progress I was making in my recovery would begin to decline. But that proved to be incorrect, and I attribute this largely to my positive attitude and the alternative treatments and therapies I sought out.

The First Three Months

The three months that I spent in the hospital were the busiest and the most intense of the entire recovery process. I received treatment from my physiotherapist, my occupational therapist, and my speech therapist on a daily basis. As it was a priority for me to regain and return to normality as quickly as possible, Pathma arranged for double sessions of physiotherapy and speech training. These were further supplemented with daily visits from our nutritionist, Alka, and our wellness therapist, Angie.

After ensuring that I had sufficient protein intake with egg whites during lunch, Alka would also carry out the qi energy balancing therapy daily before she left to return to our centre at the Adelphi. Then Angie would come in the evenings at about eight o'clock to give me a lymphatic drainage treatment with the InterX protocol that had been developed by Dr. Zulia Frost from the Neuro Resource Group in Texas.

I had first come across InterX for facial lifting treatments in 2004 when Dr. Zulia came to train our therapists at Atos Wellness. In fact, in 2002, the InterX had come to the rescue of my tired and overstrained muscles during the Prudential Bike Aid Cyclothon for a charitable cause when I had to cycle close to 150 km daily for four days in aid of the Sikh Welfare Fund. Dynamically used for post-rehabilitation by physiotherapists in Europe and the United States, the InterX continued to bring about gradual and progressive improvements in the range of motion and flexibility of my limbs.

Ayurveda

In July 2012, an Ayurvedic practitioner was consulted to assess my condition, and Abhyangam (a special herbal massage) was recommended. I started receiving these hour-long massages after the first two weeks of my stroke, and they continued for two of the three months I was in the hospital. Even when I moved back home, I continued to receive the Ayurvedic herbal massages to increase circulation, to prevent my muscles from stiffening, and to improve the general flexibility of my body. After doing this for one hour twice a week until January 2013, my body became more supple and flexible. The tightness typically found in the limbs of many stroke patients was not noticeable in mine, and I believe these massages were a contributing factor. However, I was still needing a wheelchair.

Ayurveda is one of the world's oldest medical practices. It originated in India more than 3,000 years ago and is still part of the country's standard health care. It takes into consideration the health of an individual as part of a dynamic integration with the environment, mind, body and spirit. The focus is on preservation and promotion of health and preventing the occurrence of disease. It advocates a holistic approach to understanding all aspects of human life, including diagnosis and management of disease. Ayurveda attributes primary importance to preventive medicine and the maintenance of positive health.

Acupuncture

During my stay in the hospital, my colleague Koo Ping told me of Dr. Chia Chay Puay, a doctor who specialised in acupuncture. He even offered to ferry me to Dr. Chia's clinic in Kallang Bahru two or three times a week. It was discussed with my family, and I was advised against it during my stay in the hospital because we were told that the extreme pain might result in stiffening of my muscles . We decided to stick to the conventional treatment until I was discharged. But in October 2012, I finally decided to try it out.

Dr. Chia lamented that I had not started treatment one month after my stroke, and I regretted not following his advice because I initially saw results. But when he informed me, in March 2013, that my progress had plateaued, I decided to stop treatment for the time being. However, I would definitely recommend that anyone who has suffered a stroke consider blending Western medicine with acupuncture.

Physiotherapy and Occupational Therapy

In January 2013, I also started physiotherapy and occupational therapy at Ang Mo Kio Community Hospital and Tan Tock Seng Hospital. Physiotherapy is an important part of the rehabilitation process for stroke patients because exercise, manipulation, skills training and electrical treatment (stimulating the body's electrical impulses) help us to learn to use both sides of our body again to regain as much strength and movement as possible. However, I have to admit that it was very challenging for me, as I had to relearn many basic skills that I had always taken for granted. I was inspired to improve, but my physiotherapist had to remind me to be patient.

Thankfully, I was definitely making progress, but I missed my job, and I missed my team at work. Since my health was improving while I was undergoing physiotherapy and occupational therapy, I decided to go back to work again while still continuing with the treatments. In April 2013, I started visiting my three wellness centres in my wheelchair to touch base with my customers, some of whom had been with me since we had opened. I enjoyed the interactions I had with my customers, but in July 2013, I decided to focus on my recovery full-time.

Traditional Chinese Medicine

That same month, I met with a Chinese doctor, Dr. Wong, to resume my acupuncture sessions. She would insert 150 needles into various parts of my body, literally from head to toe. She was very proficient, but unfortunately, it was too late for me. It felt like my journey to rehabilitation had started moving in another direction. One full year had passed since my stroke, and I was still needing a wheelchair. My deepest fear was that my state might be permanent! How could that happen? I was in my prime! Was it possible that I had already reached my recovery potential? The fear was very real because many people remain immobilised six to 12 months after suffering a stroke.

Acupuncture with Dr. Wong

I was not willing to accept that prognosis. I had to search harder to find ways of getting myself back to normal. I needed to do something to get back into the game, and that led me to seek out possible alternative treatments that would help me reach my goal. I was vaguely aware that such treatments existed, but I had no personal knowledge of them.

Justin Morais and Bicom Resonance Therapy

In August 2013, I was introduced by Manjit to the famous sports acupuncturist, Justin Morais. He diagnosed and worked on me with his Bicom machine that emitted therapeutic patterns of Bioresonance signals. Regular weekly sessions with Justin continued till I left for India for more intensive Ayurvedic treatments. Although these sessions proved to be rather effective, this progress spurred my determination to speed up my recovery outside Singapore.

Justin Morais

Intensive Ayurvedic Treatments in Madurai

I decided to go to the AVN Arogya Ayurvedic Hospital in Madurai for three weeks of intensive Ayurvedic therapies. It was a residential Ayurvedic treatment centre offering treatments for serious diseases, but it had the ambience of a resort. The sessions there focused on the deep massage and nourishment aspects of the nerves and provided the best care and attention, but I found it difficult to be away that long from my home and family. Here the days seemed to drag as I struggled with the pain of coming to terms with my current predicament. I decided to return to Singapore and seek other means to recover in a more familiar setting.

Upon my return from India, I resumed physiotherapy and occupational therapy until May 2015. Those had also been available to me in Madurai, but I missed the intense regular exercises I had grown used to doing on a daily basis, and I was starting to notice incremental progress in the mobility and flexibility of my muscles.

SpinoFlex Added Value to My Physiotherapy

Although I had started physiotherapy immediately after the stroke, I only began to use the SpinoFlex device, together with the treadmill, during my sessions in 2014. The device allowed me to stretch myself out while on the treadmill, and to do so safely. As there was no danger of teetering over the edge, the SpinoFlex made me more adventurous when trying out exercises that were completely out of my comfort zone. Before the SpinoFlex, I had difficulty maintaining balance, but my balance improved over a period of three years while using this device.

I was so excited that I was able to walk 30 steps! I could move my right leg forward and backward repeatedly and then do the same exercise using my left leg. With the help of the SpinoFlex, I could initially walk 300 metres in 30 minutes, but each time I was able to slowly increase my speed on the treadmill, which also helped to improve my balance.

Varma Kalai Massage

I also did Varma Kalai massage, which I had been introduced to in May of 2014. It is an ancient healing massage technique that works on acupuncture pressure points of the body called Varma points. In total, there are 108 Varma points. Various herbs, pressure methods and massage techniques are used when one of these pressure points suffers trauma. I was only able to undergo two treatments a month due to my other commitments, but I still found it to be beneficial. My flexibility and strength improved, and I continued that therapy on a regular basis.

I did not know any stroke survivors with whom I could discuss my dilemma, and this made me want to create a help line that would give fellow stroke survivors someone to lean on and to offer them advice during their recovery. I started doing research on the internet and also discussing possible treatments with friends and family. The stories I heard about stroke survivors who had recovered from their paralysed state boosted my confidence and reinforced my belief that I, too, would eventually regain my mobility. Through those success stories, I was able to learn more about alternative therapies that could support my body during my recovery. It was also then that I began to get interested and researched further into genetics testing.

Genetic Testing: My Predisposition to Inflammation Revealed

In hindsight, I highly recommend taking a genetic test. If I had taken heed of my predisposition for inflammation, I would have been able to change my diet and lifestyle to avoid my stroke or minimise the severity.

The genetic test I took three months before my stroke revealed that I had a predisposition for inflammation. Life gave me gentle hints along the way, nudging me to take some time off, create better balance, and relieve some of the pressure. Ironically, I did not take heed of my company's core value, 'Harmony from Within', and remained fixated on growing the company that became my focus. I didn't stop to take a break and reduce the amount of stress I was under. When you're at your peak, you don't just sit back and relax. It's hard work to stay at the top, juggling responsibilities, but I have learned enough in the last nine years to realise that work is not everything. My work once defined me, but I know now that it is not all that defines me. Don't make the same mistake I did. You may save yourself years of pain, anxiety, and suffering.

Interventions through Scientific Advancement

Stem cells are our body's very own matrix. We are born with them, and the human body has the ability to regenerate these cells so they can repair muscle tissue and tendons. Once in the bloodstream, adult stem cells have the ability to migrate to areas where they are most needed. This vital, life-sustaining process helps improve, maintain, and preserve our health and well-being throughout our entire lifetime. Stem cells are the core essence to life and good health.

The origins of stem cell therapy date back to the early 1800s in Switzerland, when Dr. Charles-Édouard Brown-Séquard and Dr. Paul Niehans began researching the use of animal extracts to reduce the effects of ageing.

Modern cell therapy was further legitimised in the field of bone marrow transplantation through the work of Dr. Jean Dausset, recipient of the Nobel Prize for Physiology or Medicine in 1980. His research laid much of the groundwork for the 1990 Nobel Prize recipient Dr. E. Donnall Thomas, who performed the first successful transplant of cells between identical twin patients.

I came to understand stem cells during my research, and back in 2014, I learned that I could do stem cell treatments at a medical clinic. The procedure took two days and cost S$21,000. What they did was take adipose tissue from my abdomen, extract stem cells from it, cultivate them in a lab to multiply the number of cells, and inject them back into me. I had to stay in Bangkok for two days for the doctor to assess my situation.

In August 2017, I went back again to do stem cell treatments with Dr. Kampon Sriwatanakul. All of the treatments were done in his clinic, except for a half-day procedure that was done in a hospital.

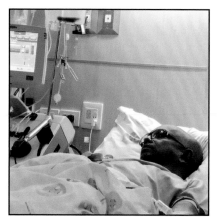

Stemcell extraction in a hospital in Thailand

Unfortunately, when I visited the doctor in Thailand three months later, I hadn't improved in the way he had expected. He said that I had started too late and that I would have experienced better results had I begun treatment immediately after my stroke.

In addition to healing my body, I embarked on my own journey of self-discovery so I could evolve beyond this lost state to forging ahead on a new path and finding clarity. It started with me finding peace by accepting that I would never have an answer to the question that had haunted me from day one: why me? There were inspiring signs all around me. I just needed to keep my mind open so I could see them.

It's difficult for me to quantify the results of these individual treatments without peer-reviewed journals, but what I can provide is an account of the various treatments that worked for my condition. However, to help you put things in perspective, I still needed a wheelchair for two years after suffering the stroke, although I did experience incremental improvement.

CHAPTER 13

A TURNAROUND

Losers quit when they fall. Winners fall until they succeed.
–Robert Kiyosaki[11]

The first few years of my rehabilitation were an immense challenge, not only for my body but also for my soul. Just after the stroke, I struggled with the psychological pain of comparing my life before and after, over and over again. In the matter of just a few minutes, I had gone from being successfully in charge of 450 people to being in charge of only myself—and barely in charge, at that! It was difficult to come to terms with such a crippling infirmity.

After spending two years needing a wheelchair, I realised that I had to move on from the mental torment to truly heal and rediscover myself. The narrative in my head needed to change, and that was made possible with the help of two people.

Dr. Darren Weissman's Half-Day Seminar and Six-Day Programme

The first was Dr. Darren Weissman, a naturopath and the developer of the LifeLine technique. On the advice of a friend, in May 2014, I attended a half-day seminar offered by Dr. Weissman. He spoke extensively about the power of infinite love and gratitude. For me, viewing life that way had always come naturally, but the stroke had forced me to confront my own beliefs about the inherent goodness of things.

Dr. Weissman had such an impact that I decided to follow up and attend a six-day seminar that August in Adelaide. There were about 60 participants, the majority of whom were already working in the healing profession as chiropractors, yoga instructors, or wellness therapists, and some had come for a refresher. Through individual and collective healing sessions, we were exposed to in-depth experiential learning.

Dr. Weissman imparted to us the skills required to facilitate a LifeLine session for ourselves and others. Feelings of confusion and denial bubbled up within me; those feelings were foreign to me. As Dr. Weissman shared his beliefs about infinite love and gratitude toward everything in our lives, whether we perceive them as good or bad, memories of how I used to be trickled back and filled me with a different energy.

I was suddenly open to seeing the bigger picture. It was as though something inside of me clicked. The realisation hit me: I could change a negative event into a positive one simply by changing my outlook. Dr. Weissman's way of looking at my situation left me feeling like there must have been a bigger, more important reason for my stroke. But what? Could it be that I was meant to share my experience for the benefit of others? Was that my gift? Still, it wasn't clear how I would do that. I was not meeting many people at that time. The rehabilitation process kept me preoccupied, but I was now open to understanding the deeper purpose that could emerge from my stroke, and that put me in a better position to come to terms with my disability.

I realised that all of the times that I had asked myself 'why me?' only dampened my spirits and held me back. Now I finally reached a point where I could begin to truly reflect on my circumstances and accept that my stroke was not entirely detrimental. It could, in fact, be seen as a blessing in disguise or, as Dr. Weissman put it so succinctly, 'a gift in strange wrapping paper.'

A New Beginning

The stroke was a horrific experience that derailed my life, but being able to feel love and gratitude for the people who carried me through the experience could indeed unveil something beautiful within me. The immediate rush I experienced felt like a release of sorts. The bulk of the negative sentiments fell away, and in their place, I filled my heart with love and thankfulness while embracing my current situation.

After Dr. Weissman's LifeLine programme, I knew my life was going to take a new direction. I suddenly had a deep desire to accomplish something for myself, and I knew what I had to do—I had to write a book about my experience. Yes, I may have run my own company for 30 years, but for the first time in my life, I felt like *I* was the one in control. When I returned to Singapore, I felt empowered and filled with a renewed focus to make my experience a platform that would enable others who had experienced a life event like mine to be helped and experience success.

Trevor Gollagher's Personal Mentoring Sessions

The second person who surpassed my expectations and changed the trajectory of my recovery was Trevor Gollagher. After Dr. Weissman's seminar, I attended Trevor's personal mentoring programme, which consisted of 10 weekly sessions that lasted about 45 minutes each. These sessions were conducted one-on-one via Skype. Trevor worked with me to expose the negative conditioning of my past. Then, through seeking to overcome this conditioning, we set the intent to live more purposefully.

Trevor explained that people often move through life in a state of unconsciousness. They don't understand the bigger purpose behind the various setbacks that they experience. Coupled with their own perceptions and limiting belief systems, they then create and experience a false reality, which gives rise to the perception that adversity will lead them downhill. However, if we manage to stave off such a feeling, it will fade away and eventually cease to exist. This, however, is difficult to achieve, and requires that we learn to view our experiences through a different lens.

According to Trevor, every experience, whether perceived as positive or negative, is meant to expand our soul's consciousness. This helps an individual to be better able to accept the inevitable knocks of life and opens the doorway to positive outcomes. Through living a life of 'flow', or nonresistance, one is able to defuse the tension that creates inflammation on the mental, emotional, physical and spiritual levels.

His reference to inflammation sent a jolt through me. The Fitgenes test I had undergone prior to my stroke indicated that my body was predisposed to inflammation. That made me reflect upon the various areas of my life and the situations where I could have been resisting, and it paved the way for me to improve in specific areas. *What am I resisting?* Slowly, I came to the point of not seeking to change my experiences, but rather to feel love within each experience, knowing that each one is a vital part of my soul's journey of expansion. Even the terrible experience of the stroke was meant for my soul's expansion. Working with Trevor helped me to gain a deeper insight into what Dr. Weissman had earlier shared about how every life experience is actually a gift.

Trevor also emphasised that every single thing that happens in our lives is part of God's—or the universe's if you prefer—perfect plan for us. Having this perspective helps an individual be more open to *experiencing* rather than *opposing* life's currents.

One of the positive effects of these sessions was my change of heart with regard to work. Before, I had not considered going back to business at all. I believed that this stage of my life was over. However, all of that changed after the programme, when I learned that the pace of recovery is inextricably linked to the patient's effort to lead a purposeful life. That gave me the inspiration to begin working again.

CHAPTER 14

COMING TO TERMS WITH MY CONDITION

The whole of life is coming to terms with yourself and the natural world.
Why are you here? How do you fit in? What is it all about?

–David Attenborough[12]

The guidance of Dr. Darren Weissman and Trevor Gollagher helped to accelerate my recovery because, for the first time, I truly believed that I could get better. Both programmes helped me recognise and deal with various limiting factors in my subconscious that affected my motivation to live a full life again.

Neuroplasticity

The human brain possesses a wonderful natural ability to reorganise itself after enormous trauma. They call this *neuroplasticity*. In response to damage from disease or injury, the nerve cells in the brain respond by adjusting themselves. They build bridges in the form of new neural connections to replace the old ones.

While most improvements generally happen within three to six months of the illness, the presence of neuroplasticity meant that my body would conspire with me to make continuous improvements but *only* as long as I persevered. I simply needed to reposition my state of mind to allow the healing to happen. This was where Dr. Weissman's programme was important.

I was already aware of this natural phenomenon when Dr. Weissman spoke of it at the seminar, and now I began to research how I could harness it to improve myself.

Neuroplasticity drove my path forward in my determination to come to terms with my condition and to do whatever it takes to get my body back to as close to normalcy as I possibly could. There was no holding back my thirst for knowledge and experimentation. This search propelled me into an extensive and expensive journey to places I never knew existed and introduced me to experts with obscure inventions based upon science rather than popularly accepted mainstream medicine.

My journey's discoveries were many, and I shall put forth in this and subsequent chapters what I personally tried. I shall also share my thoughts and introduce the many products and therapies I went through while seeking for the best solutions for my condition. As I had said, I would do anything and everything to get well. I would suggest that you understand the sincerity with which I share these experiences with the intention of opening up possibilities that you—my reader—may find useful. It was when I found that there was nothing available that I could go to that I sought out these on my own. I am in no way advocating or endorsing any of what I had tried. All I do here is share what I went through and what I found useful in my journey toward rehabilitation.

Needing a Wheelchair-No Longer!

My first goal was to do away with the wheelchair. After relying on it for two years, my morale had taken a dive.

Now that I realised it was indeed possible, I kept saying firmly to myself, 'Aanandha, we have to get rid of the wheelchair!'

An image sprung to mind. It was the memory of my physiotherapist gently nagging me in the hospital: 'Aanandha, it's very important that you psych yourself up so that you will eventually give up the wheelchair!'

More memories surfaced of my wife and daughters prodding me to get out of the wheelchair. So many people were on my side. Why did I start to think that I was doing this alone?

I renewed my efforts in earnest. I made myself get out of the wheelchair and, with assistance, shuffle along on my own two legs for as far as I could go. Initially, I could only walk one hundred metres aided, but over time, I could walk for longer stretches as my stamina increased. What a marvellous thing, this neuroplasticity! The more I learned about the human body, the more it seemed like a miracle unto itself. It was like proof of the improbable, and it fuelled my desire to learn more and discover more.

Every month, I improved my walking range as well as my balance. Then my speech and cognitive functions followed suit. The improvements were significant enough that my friends began to remark on the difference. For the first time in a long time, I could truly see the possibility that I would one day walk on my own.

Success Stories That Motivated Me!

I also drew encouragement from other success stories, like the case of a neuroscientist named Jill Bolte. Jill eventually recovered from her stroke after persisting for eight years, and she credited neuroplasticity for her recovery. Other stories spoke of those who had gradually recovered from a stroke after 10 years or more.

As I compared what I read with what I experienced, I quickly discovered that the natural healing process could be enhanced if it was combined with exercise. Then I trained under Dr. Rano Rahmat, PhD, who had successfully combined acupuncture with exercise.

In July 2014, I visited Dr. Rano at the Changi General Hospital (CGH) in Singapore after he was hospitalised for a stroke that was brought on by excess stress. He had previously been a very adept *silat* (Malay martial arts) instructor, and he had a PhD in sports fitness. We had met twice before, but when I heard about his predicament through a friend, I was eager to meet with him and lend my support. But when I saw him in his hospital bed, he was unable to speak and did not appear to recognise me.

When I next saw Dr. Rano in September 2015, I was amazed at his rapid recovery. Even though my stroke had occurred in 2012, I still could not walk independently by 2015. Dr. Rano, on the other hand, had experienced a full recovery, except for his speech, which was not yet fully restored. He was able to recount how the doctors had initially given him a poor prognosis after his haemorrhagic stroke. He had suffered extensive brain damage with a five-centimetre lesion in the prefrontal lobe. The doctors were concerned with the extent of the bleed in his brain, and they thought it would be very difficult for him to recover his faculties. But he defied expectation.

Dr. Rano credits his recovery to being able to perform acupuncture treatments on himself starting one month after he suffered his stroke. As an acupuncture practitioner, he had instinctively known that it was best not to wait too long before beginning the treatment. So, after his first 30 days at the hospital, he asked his doctors for permission to check out for the weekend and return home. There, he would perform intramuscular acupuncture treatments on himself. He did so without informing the doctors, and he understood that he was taking his own professional risk. Afterward, he would return to the hospital to continue his regular treatment. As the nerves in the brain stem started to activate, he began combining his treatment with gradual physical exercise, which created a positive feedback loop in the brain that accelerated his success.

Dr. Rano described leaving the hospital on a Friday for the weekend and returning that Sunday able to walk on his own. Needless to say, his doctors were amazed! There is even a video of Dr. Rano in the CGH taken a few months after his stroke, showing his rapid recovery because of acupuncture.

Dr. Rano shared with me that both acupuncture and active exercise were the perfect combination for such dramatic results. He then told me that he could help me in my recovery, and I was very excited about the possibilities. Also, I was thrilled when I first heard about his gym, since I did not realise that I could go to the gym after my stroke. My physiotherapists had never discussed that option as a means of working on my muscles. I had no fear of this, however, as I implicitly trusted in Dr. Rano's expertise, especially after such a powerful testimony.

My Workout at the Gym

A few days later, I went to the gym for the first time after the stroke. It was an eye-opener. While the others were exercising to build their bodies, I was there trying to prevent mine from collapsing. We first did 30 minutes of vibration training to improve my balance, followed by weights and other exercises. Then I continued at the gym twice a week with each session lasting about an hour. We used the vertical vibration plate, leg press, leg extension, squats, hamstring curl, chest press, lat pulldown, shoulder press, elliptical row and step board. I realised that my leg and arm muscles could be steadily strengthened. Within only two weeks, I could see a marked improvement in my muscles, and the wonderful bonus was that my mind was *clearer*!

Vibration Training with Dr. Rano

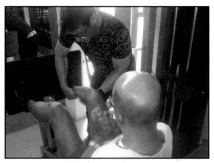

Workout at the gym

Strengthening my arms

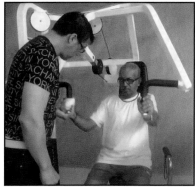

Pushing hard

It made me hopeful that I could still achieve greater muscle tone through targeted exercises, and with more training, I have continued to improve over time. I've come so far since then, and I continue to set new targets and seek out other therapies to increase the neuroplasticity of my brain.

While it is extremely important for stroke patients to exercise in order to stimulate and strengthen weakened muscles, I learned from both Justin Morais's and Dr. Rano's experiences the importance of including cellular therapies to enhance the body's self-healing abilities, particularly in the brain. That inspired me to try the German Biological Cell Regulation (BCR) Therapie.

Biological Cell Regulation

The BCR system originated when its German developers realised that the microcurrent system could be vastly improved by flowing electric currents both ways and changing frequencies, pulse, and polarity and by incorporating bio-cybernetics technology, or autodetection and response capabilities, which is a form of artificial intelligence.

Inspired by Dr. Voll's theory of linking bioelectrical measurements to the pathology in the body, the diagnosis in BCR systems enables the use of measurements of bioelectrical impedance in administering treatments to cause changes to the impedance toward its optimum level so that the body is able to self-heal and self-repair the affected tissue or organ. These treatments are built into its algorithms and are automated into the system.

It is said that when the body is suffering from injury, infection, or inflammation, cell metabolism is seen to be in disorder locally or systemically throughout the whole body. This disorder weakens the body's self-healing ability. This is something I picked up—that if we supported our bodies with what is critical for it to work well, the body is able to heal itself. This is where exercise, proper nutrition and relaxation are key supports to be infused into our daily lives. In this light, the BCR system is built to help the body's disrupted cell chemistry and enable its self-healing qualities to correct its 'system' rather than to treat the 'symptoms'.

It was no surprise thus that I purchased the BCR system called the Luxxamed and began to slowly see some effects. Before I started the BCR treatment on a daily basis, I found my right leg often rigid. As time went by, my leg became more flexible, and I found it easier to enter into the taxis that I often used to commute around.

Hydrotherapy Home Spa

One year after my stroke, a friend told me that hydrotherapy at home would be able to help me with my recovery. My brother, Sri, had a home spa device that he sent to me. Unfortunately, I was not able to use the hydrotherapy spa as I was not able to get into the tub. My inflexible body did not allow me to get into the tub until three years later, in 2016, when I was finally able to do so with the assistance of my helper. Now, I do hydrotherapy at least once a day. I would recommend that anyone over the age of 40 get themselves a hydrotherapy home spa as it is very therapeutic.

I liken the SG2000 Ultrasonic Hydrotherapy Home Spa to what is achieved after a vigorous 30-minute exercise routine. You can feel the heat being emitted from within your body. The internal warming increases one's body temperature and thus boosts the immune system and metabolic rate. Increased cellular activity also raises energy levels and improves the delivery of nutrients and oxygen to the organs, while removing metabolic waste through perspiration.

Kenkoh Sandals

It wasn't just the intensive treatments and lengthy seminars that had a positive impact on me; sometimes it was the little things that impacted my recovery. In 2016, I noticed an interesting pair of sandals in the pharmacy, and I was told by staff that they were Kenkoh sandals from Japan. They looked different from typical sandals because they had nodules that were designed to have a massaging effect on your feet. I purchased a pair for $80, but when I returned home and tried to use them, I found it difficult to walk with them on. It took me about two weeks before I was able to slowly inch my way along the floor wearing the sandals; but after six months, I was able to walk in the sandals for at least half an hour every day. I am sure you have heard that foot reflexology has a therapeutic effect on the whole body. With the concept of neuroplasticity, I felt that this constant engagement of my nerves at my feet with my Kenkoh sandals enabled me to walk better and further, as the constant massaging of my feet while walking was clearly beneficial.

AmLife

It was in August 2016 when I came to know about the AmLife mattress. Often at 4 a.m., I would awaken from sleep no matter what time I got to bed. My difficulty of having a good night's sleep was something that bothered me even before the stroke. I was advised to use the AmLife for two to three hours in the day and during the night as well.

I was told that AmLife is scientifically designed to maximise our body's natural healing mechanism by promoting cell regeneration, apart from other positive outcomes. Both its functions of providing electric potential and infrared therapies come from Japanese technology with more than 50 years of testing and experimentation. I started using AmLife in the hope that I would have better sleep.

Scalp Acupuncture

In December 2017, I crossed paths again with Dr. Chua Eng Khong. We had first met through the Singapore National Stroke Association (SNSA) when he came to present about scalp acupuncture that had been developed in America by Professor Zhu Ming Qing.

On 24 November 1987, Professor Zhu had demonstrated an innovative acupuncture technique on a hemiplegic stroke patient (a patient paralysed on one side of the body) at the first International Conference of Acupuncture and Moxibustion in Beijing. After the treatment, the patient had stood up and moved around without support. Professor Zhu had garnered much international recognition since that day.

Dr. Chua told me that Professor Zhu felt that it was never too late for scalp acupuncture to help a stroke patient in their recovery, so Dr. Chua started coming to my home once a week to perform treatments that lasted between 90 minutes and two hours. The difference between the treatments performed by Dr. Chua and other acupuncturists was that Dr. Chua spent at least an hour working with me on physical therapy and balance. He then left the acupuncture needles in for three days.

It was unfortunate that he was the only doctor in Singapore who had been trained by Professor Zhu. There is a lot of information on scalp acupuncture, and I feel that it is very important that this form of acupuncture be practiced by more acupuncture doctors in Singapore and globally.

Varma Kalai Revisited

In early 2018, I met Raja Mohan, an expert who was trained deep in the Indian mountains by a Varma Kalai master. *Varma Kalai* is an ancient Indian term meaning 'the art of vital points.' This healing science originated thousands of years ago in Tamil Nadu. Its components are used in traditional massage, alternative medicine, traditional yoga and martial arts. The body's pressure points (Varma points) are manipulated to heal or to cause harm.

Through him, I learned about the inner wisdom of Varma Kalai therapy, an age-old, specialised form of martial art used by Indian warriors of the past. It teaches how to return to the battlefield, fit and ready to fight, after an injury. Varma Kalai–style therapy gave me renewed confidence during a time when I would consistently plateau.

Ancient Varma Kalai with Raja Mohan and Greg Watters

"Because we all have to deal with a lot of daily stress, we can tend to shut down the energy flow to certain parts of the body because of emotional issues, overwork, poor nutrition, or not enough sleep, and this results in sore necks and shoulders, and stomach issues,' says Raja Mohan. 'Working with the vital points restores the energy flow to the affected area, which removes any energetic blockage and allows the body to come back into balance once again."[13]

I have been doing Varma Kalai weekly with Raja Mohan, and it is making my body stronger and more flexible. More information on Raja Mohan and Varma Kalai can be found in Appendix 3 on page 185.

It was Raja Mohan who introduced me to yoga instructor Greg Watters, who then figured out how I could perform yoga in my limited physical state. I have documented the various yoga protocols that Greg Watters taught my helper so she could work with me weekly. Greg and I still practise the various stretches that continue to keep my joints and muscles more supple and flexible.

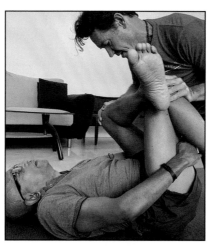

Yoga with Greg Watters

Herbal Medicine

It was in 2013 that I met Linda Bates. She is a traditional herbalist, a nutritional biochemist, and an experienced clinician who primarily worked with people with special diets, herbal medicines, and sometimes supplements. When I first spoke to Linda, it was when I was working hard at getting my right side of my body reconnected to my brain so that I could walk and use my right arm again.

According to Linda, damaged nerves that were cut off from their connection to the brain—which is their control centre—have a unique kind of sensation, a very deep ache. New nerves have to be grown and reconnected. Circulation has to be restored, and new peripheral blood vessels have to be encouraged to grow. All of this takes medicinally active ingredients that are only available in herbs. Her prescription together with the physical and structural treatments and exercise regimes would give me repair that happened faster.

This made sense to me, and I quickly went about placing orders with Linda for my pain relief and circulation- and nerve-restoring herbal mixes. However, I did not follow up on these after they ended and unfortunately lost touch with Linda till early June 2020. This time, I was given herbs to take internally to support further repair alongside my programme of exercise, physio, and acupuncture with creams to restore and strengthen my joints. She also gave me a diet for recovery tailored for me.

It was only in 2020 that I fully realised the power of herbs, as I now feel connected with the knowledge she gave me on herbal medicine. My faith grew in these as my mind began to extend its capacity to engage better with information that came my way.

It may seem to you a little confusing that I had tried so many modalities with so many diverse applications and concoctions. You may also wonder if all these had indeed worked for me to settle the issues that I continue to face. What I would say to you is it is a synergistic combination of stimulation to my body that keeps me active and alert. My body is still being fine-tuned to reach a new normal state that will help reengineer a new me, more independent in mind and body.

Over the years, after my paradigm shift in viewing my stroke as a gift, I now look at my life with hope and renewed confidence. Thoughts that once plagued me with questions now reflect my forward-looking perspective. Happily, my heart and mind are now in sync after coming to terms with my condition.

With this milestone shift in gears in my mind, my journey became more driven in seeking an all-or-nothing approach toward rebuilding myself from scratch.

CHAPTER 15

IT ALL STARTS WITH NUTRITION

Our food should be our medicine and our medicine should be our food.

–Hippocrates

Back to my inner boardroom, my fingers shifted toward the search for Google in my iPhone. These became my constant companions during the day as I searched with keywords for anything related to stroke and recovery. This led me to seek different routes for my same driven goal. Though I had come to terms with my conditions, I was not willing to accept it—that I had plateaued.

I lived this new 'plateau' while I researched voraciously everywhere, from friends' word-of-mouth solutions to taxi drivers' sharing of their stories toward recovery. I realised that rebuilding meant a whole host of lifestyle makeovers from within.

It all starts with nutrition! My searches led me toward the importance of nutrition. This brought me back to those days in 1995.

The Importance of Nutrition

Back in 1995, my industrial cleaning business in Singapore was floundering, and my friend Manjit Singh suggested that I consider becoming a vegetarian for two weeks because things might change for the better. What did I have to lose?

I went to the Sai Baba Ashram in Puttaparthi, South India. There, I meditated every day while observing a vegetarian diet. Astonishingly, just as Manjit had suggested, things did start to change after my return. Opportunities opened up, and I established my very first wellness centre that year.

I kept up with the daily programme of vegetarianism and meditation to ensure those changes would last. Where health was concerned, I falsely believed vegetarianism gave me some sort of immunity and that the diet of high carbohydrates and low protein would fortify me against serious illness. At the time, I was young and strong, my mind was clear, and my body was vibrant with energy. Fast-forward 15 years, and my vitality had started to wane without my noticing it.

In hindsight, my approach to health and diet was definitely not the best; it may even have contributed to my stroke. Eating out became a convenience, and I was eating highly processed mock meat (any vegetarian food made to resemble a meat product) that contained gluten and processed salt. As a vegetarian, I thought that I would be protected against having any serious health problems, particularly arteriosclerosis (thickening of arterial walls, often restricting blood flow) or heart problems. I now know that this is not true. As a vegetarian, you can be less healthy than someone who eats meat, and you can still have high blood pressure, inflammation, diabetes, anaemia, migraines, low energy, and stress-related disorders.

Theories of Nutrition

I realise that there is a huge amount of information on nutrition, but it's not always easy to find reliable information. There are many different theories about what you should or shouldn't consume—low fat, vegetarian, Pritikin, ketogenic, paleo, and many others. Each one claims to be the best, and it can be difficult to decide what constitutes healthy eating, what is best for your particular body, and what is best when it comes to particular health issues.

However, if you can buy fresh fish, that is a much better choice than heavy meats. Sourcing fresh and clean ocean or river fish can be a challenge, especially in countries that rely on imports. Many of our waterways are polluted, so the fish and seafood we eat might contain metals, plastics, oil, radiation and other pollutants.

Personally, since my brush with death, the effort I made to understand the importance of nutrition and how to have a successful vegetarian lifestyle led me toward Dr. Bruce Lipton, the best-selling author of *Biology of Belief*.

He is famous for his work in epigenetics (the study of heritable changes caused by the activation and deactivation of genes, not changes in DNA sequence) and neurobiology (the study of brain and nerve function), and he has researched how our emotions and mental state affect our genes. You *become* those thoughts you put the most focus on each day.

I mention Dr. Lipton because his discoveries have been instrumental in my recovery. Using his techniques has helped me to push my mind to improve my rehabilitation beyond what is considered normal. My body had become so dysfunctional that my mind was all I had left to work with. Luckily, mental power has been one of my great strengths. It just seemed natural to employ positive thoughts and willpower to help me get back on my feet.

According to Dr. Lipton, 'the way cells function demonstrates the existence of God.'[14] As a spiritual person, that makes absolute sense to me. If we believe, as I do, that God is everywhere, both inside and out, then the divine force is at our disposal. So, away I went, employing Dr. Lipton's mind concepts with gusto to unlock the healing genes within.

His theories also extend to food. He talks a lot about the emotions we normally associate with eating particular things, such as chocolate cake, ice cream, or chips. Now, when I do indulge in a little culinary decadence, I focus on enjoying every mouthful and associating the experience with positive emotions. It is incredible how much better it feels and how smoothly my body assimilates this heavier food—no bloating, no upset stomach, no sugar slump, and no guilt.

What Is the Ultimate Diet?

The questions most people ask are, is there an ultimate diet, and if so, what is it? Dr. Lipton, along with most dieticians, would say that there's no such thing because everyone has a different body type and different physiology. There's no one-size-fits-all solution. There are, however, some general guidelines. Nutritional science says we should eat to only 75 percent capacity—in other words, until we feel three-quarters full. If we can achieve that, it will allow us to lead a more fruitful, energetic and balanced life. How do you do that? The trick is not to eat until you feel full but only until you're no longer hungry. It takes some practice, but it can be done.

A healthy diet also draws from each of the five food groups—vegetables, grains, fruits, nuts, and fats. Your plate should be full of colour and various tastes. Ayurvedic medicine suggests every meal should contain six tastes: sweet, sour, salty, bitter, pungent, and astringent. I decided to incorporate some of these into my diet—something I had never done in my life.

My Nutrition Plan

First thing in the morning, prior to meditation, I do deep breathing. After meditation and 20 minutes of light exercise, I have freshly squeezed lemon water and 10 ml of apple cider vinegar. That ensures that if my pH (potential/power of hydrogen) is out of balance from eating food the night before, my stomach will quickly be brought back into balance by the apple cider vinegar. In the morning, I eat fruits and then vegetables. Daily, I eat raisins, nuts and seeds. On some days, I have oats mixed with fruits and vegetables.

My breakfast　　　　*My lunch*　　　　*My dinner*

For lunch, I have quinoa with several types of vegetables and tofu. And for dinner, it's buckwheat soba noodles with either raw or steamed vegetables. Occasionally, I will eat eggs. My diet is about 50 percent raw and 50 percent cooked.

Today, I have a complete vegetarian diet. I eat little mock meat, rarely any take-out food, and I eat organic whenever possible. I can remain a vegetarian as long as I am able to replace the nutrients in my diet that one ordinarily gets from meat. I take a few supplements to ensure my body gets the right oils, including omega-3, -6, and -9, as well as vitamin B12. I take a sublingual form of vitamin B12, which means that I place a drop of liquid or a tablet under my tongue. Those nutrients are vital for healthy nerve, tissue, brain, and red blood cell function. Vegetarians can eat butter, mushrooms, cheese and avocados to ensure that they are getting the recommended daily allowances. Some (like me) include eggs. My challenge then was to determine if what I ate reached my cells.

Nutrition Absorption

My life today is about balance, and that is why nutrition is so important. Getting nutrients to the body is pretty easy. You simply have to grab a carrot and eat it, but what happens to the carrot after that? Don't worry; I had never thought about it either. When you are under stress, the body will not work properly and will not absorb the nutrients you put into it. It does the same thing with water. If your body is full of anxiety and toxins, it won't absorb water as effectively.

Nutrient absorption starts in the mouth, not the gut. Nutritionists will lecture you on mastication and warn you about the dangers of gulping down a meal as you rush from one meeting to the next. But no busy business person wants to hear that because we fear it will slow us down. A wise person once said to me, 'Aanandha, life is a marathon, not a sprint.' Learn from my mistake. Sprinting too hard almost cost me my life. It put me in the hospital and took a huge toll on my family.

Nutrition absorption is also compromised when one's busy and stressful lifestyle is further complicated with one's genetic predisposition. In my case, my predisposition to inflammation provided me valuable information to manage my lifestyle such that my quality of life is enhanced.

Today, I know that there are certain teas and spices, like turmeric, that can reduce inflammation in the body, while excessive salt, fried food, sugar, and LDL (low-density lipoprotein) cholesterol can increase inflammation. I now know what to avoid. Meditation, yoga, breathing, and light exercise are also a good way to alkalise the body after a hard day at the office.

I became aware of sugar, as it raises the body's acidity levels. Consumption of fizzy drinks, canned juices, chocolate bars and candy should be kept to a minimum. If you experience cravings, try introducing magnesium into your daily diet. Overall, homegrown food is the best. Organic food is great, but if you can grow some vegetables at home, nothing beats fresh food plucked from your garden or your balcony.

Refined sugar and chemically processed salt are harmful to our bodies, but sea salt and Himalayan or bamboo salt are great. Unlike refined salt, they contain important trace minerals that are good for the body. Salt in moderation is good for you, but not table salt.

Healthy Food Preparation Makes Sense!

Equally as important as what food you eat is how you prepare your food. The best way to cook yams, sweet potatoes, pumpkin, or beetroot is by roasting them with the skin on in organic grass-fed butter. Add some sea salt, garlic, or chilli for spice. I have found that the best way to retain nutrients when cooking food is *sous vide* or pressure cooking, which retains 90–95 percent of nutrients. Oven roasting or steaming retains up to 90 percent, followed by stir-fried and deep-fried. Boiling reduces nutrients by up to 60 percent.

There is such a thing as healthy deep-fried food. The Japanese have been doing it for hundreds of years, and they call it *tempura*. The oil you choose is the key to healthier deep frying. If you use avocado oil, rice bran oil, or other oils with a high smoke point, then the food will be reasonably healthy. That is because those oils do not break down at high heat to become rancid.

Food for Thought

If you ever question whether or not you can change your diet and nutrition habits, consider the story of Ming Jye, who inspired me after my stroke and proved how the mind can heal the body.

The Story of Ming Jye

Back in 2008, I was at a food court with my family when I saw a grossly overweight man about 10 metres away using sign language to communicate with his friends. I went over and tried to talk to him, but realised that he was deaf. I wrote on the back of my business card, 'I can help you to lose weight.' He looked startled, but he took my card, and I rejoined my family.

The following Monday, I received a call from a Mr. Koh Piak Chong, who was the father of Ming Jye, and he asked if they could both meet with me. It turned out that Ming Jye had been overweight since he was young. He had tried to lose weight but hadn't been successful.

Ming Jye, age 26, began coming to our centre three times a week, and I gave him protein shakes and put him on a slimming programme that would help him lose weight. He was more than 200 kg at that time, but with the help of the Atos team, he lost 114 kg in two and a half years. That's about 1 kg a week, which is a very safe way to lose weight. There were times when Ming Jye found it difficult to carry on, but the constant encouragement from the team supported his weight loss, and that made a difference in his life.

Ming Jye in 2008 *Ming Jye and his father in 2011*

Nutrition Supplementation Has a Role

It was my belief in nutrition supplementation that drew me to seek essential nutrition for the cells. I had introduced spirulina and royal jelly in the early years of Atos in 1991.

Later in mid-1990s, I imported the Health Diet and The Natural Way.

It was in early 2010 when I met Professor Wang, who introduced me to microalgae and Peroxisome Proliferator-Activated Receptors (PPARS). We brought in Vital Essence as I felt that such nutrients for the cells are so important for one's health and vitality. Luckily, I began a regime of cellular nutrition. When I was struck by my stroke in 2012, nutrition also played a major role in my continued recovery.

I soon began to take 40 Vital Essence tablets daily. As nutrition supplementation became particularly necessary to counter the various challenges along the food chain due to climatic change, pollution, and commercial malpractices in food production, it came as no surprise when I introduced other nutrients to my company. Thus in 2019, we brought in Gene Activa, an energised blend of freeze-dried super fruits and vegetables with its unique formulation of Swiss apple stem cells.

Thus, my search led me to meet several CEOs, inventors, and scientists from many countries with their curated products unique in each of their own ways. I went through several affiliate marketing products.

From 2014 to 2021, I had spent eight years investigating affiliate market strategies and products. I had purchased approximately $2,000 worth of products a month on various supplements, which are mentioned in this chapter.

My sharing here captured most of what I had invested, and I am certain I must have benefited from these supplements that have enhanced my level of wellness as, even today, I get comments of surprise over my constant improvements from the last time my friends and acquaintances saw me.

Stem Cell Supplementation: An Alternative to Invasive Stem Cell Procedures

Stem Cell Worx (SCW)

My interest in stem cell supplementation increasingly grew after my stroke. It was in 2014 that I chanced across a supplement called Stem Cells Worx. It contains bovine colostrum, trans-resveratrol, and fucoidan. My research further brought me to a conclusion that their formulation naturally activates one's own adult stem cells, forming an alternative to invasive stem cell procedures.

As my experimentation with varying products increased, I started switching products once every three to six months as I didn't want my body to become adapted to the product. That would reduce its effectiveness. I decided also to space out the various supplements so that I could take them individually over a three to six month period.

Stem Enhance Ultra (SEU)

In 2017, I was looking for stem cell support and heard about SEU, which had to be purchased from Australia. I used SEU for about six months at a time. It supports your body's natural release of bone marrow stem cells.

Through multiple clinical trials, SEU was documented to optimise stem cell function in the body by increasing the number of both stem cells and endothelial progenitor cells in the blood circulation supporting optimum renewal and repair of tissues and organs.

SEU is a concentrate that combines extracts from nature's most primitive superfoods, water microalgae and marine macroalgae, providing the body with stem cell support. It contains Aphanizomenon flos-aquae concentrate (AFA), Mesenkine (spirulina platensis extract), and fucoidan (Undaria pinnatifida extract).

RevitaBlu

It was in 2013 after my stroke that I met the pioneer in stem cell research, Dr. Christian Drapeau, who was behind the product RevitaBlu, which was introduced to the world in 2019. After I had read deeply into his research, I decided to try the product, which is a botanical blend of blue-green algae, sea buckthorn berry, and aloe vera with coconut water powder.

ASEA: Ground-Breaking Research

When I found my energy constantly sapping as my days filled with therapies that were in place to aid in my recovery process, I started taking ASEA in December 2017. This came about as I read further into what is called 'redox signalling'. This describes the way the cells in our bodies function. Our ability to stay healthy and to have more energy with greater vitality relies on how well our cells function. Redox signalling is a cellular message that helps protect, rejuvenate and restore cells.

When we are young and in good health, our cells typically operate at virtually perfect efficiency, producing essential energy for the rest of the body and repairing themselves whenever needed. As we age, our cells become less efficient, with a constant bombardment by free radicals and toxins being the norm. This results in damaged, distressed, and poorly functioning cells, which translates to an imbalanced state of overall health.

What is interesting in ASEA is that this problem can now be addressed, as a group of medical professionals, engineers, and researches have discovered a proprietary method for creating and stabilising molecules native to the human body. This created the foundational technology behind ASEA, which provided a way to deliver to the body these stabilised redox-signalling molecules that are necessary for optimal cellular health. These are necessary for the performance of antioxidants that have to be 'turned on' or activated before they can do their job of neutralising free radicals.

Fountain of Life: The Healing Nature of Spruce

In August 2018, I was introduced to Fountain of Life, an extract from the Norwegian spruce tree with antioxidant and anti-inflammatory properties. There is a lot of research on the importance of lignans, which are polyphenols found in plants. A recent French study, conducted over seven years with 58,049 women, concluded that high dietary intake of plant lignans correlated with better health. Also, a 30-year study in Finland demonstrated that dietary lignans support heart health.[15]

For those who prefer not to take consumption products, I found these three companies that had very good products.

doTERRA: The Health Benefits of Essential Oils

In 2018, I started using essential oils from doTERRA for about one year. At that time, I did not know that essential oils are very important to bringing the body into balance. It was only in 2020 that I came to know that essential oils have been used for more than 3,000 years. I began using their blends, and my favourites are the Adaptive Calming Blend and Lavender Peace for a good night's sleep.

Firmax3

I found that Firmax3, a cream that contains hydrolysed marine collagen, apple stem cell extract, tongkat ali root extract, manjakani oak gall extract, sausage tree fruit extract, and liquorice root extract, helped to improve my circulation.

R3R

I found this company, which originates from Singapore. I had a chance meeting with the owner, Ernie Chu, and asked him why he started R3R, which is in many Asian countries. He said he wanted to create opportunities for countless individuals around the globe.

The R3R cleanser is unique in that it uses encapsulation technology and uses apple stem cells from the Uttwiler Spätlauber apple tree. Other ingredients are papaya enzymes, pineapple enzymes, and hyaluronic acid.

Revolutions behind Products

New products keep coming into our market consistently. Today nutrition is a trillion-dollar business, and consumers are now spoilt for choice. My word of advice here is to thoroughly research every product that comes your way for its veracity and validity. For many, these are a means of business, and thus before investing in any of these, investigate all claims closely and do the necessary due diligence before embarking on any investment of time or money. That was when I decided on ASEA, doTERRA, and Firmax, both as a business and for their healing properties.

Frankly, this research only happened as a result of my current condition. I would never have had the time nor drive to persevere through such a journey through life the way I have done in pursuit of therapeutic products and therapies. Stress—with its adrenaline and cortisol by-products—forced me to realise the need to manage it on a daily basis. I felt the urgency to dedicate one chapter of my book to stress management in the hope that this becomes routinised in everyone's lives.

CHAPTER 16

DISARMING THE SILENT KILLER

I will breathe.
I will think of solutions.
I will not let my worry control me.
I will not let my stress break me.
I will simply breathe, and it will be okay because I don't quit.

—Shayne McClendon[16]

We live in trying times. The collective stress of people is palpable. Many of us carry the fear of death, crime, terrorism, old age, rejection and failure.

Just before my stroke in 2012, our holding company was at its peak, and I was in a race to outrun myself. When I recall how I operated during those days, the phrase 'in the zone' springs to mind. I was so often in my head that I didn't give my body, heart, or overall well-being a second thought. I was not conscious of my health, and as the CEO of a wellness company, it's deeply embarrassing and humbling to have suffered the way I have. I arrogantly thought that because things were going so well, I could not fall. I ignored the messages from my body and mind, and they combined to teach me a very valuable lesson.

Stress: The Silent Killer! How?

Is stress a silent killer? That's the question I should have been asking myself years before my stroke. Looking back through the rearview mirror, the answer is an emphatic 'yes'.

There are a lot of things that you probably don't know about stress. If you constantly run on adrenaline, you will suffer from adrenal fatigue. If you don't recognise the signs and make sensible changes to your lifestyle, the next symptoms could be chronic fatigue and neurological degeneration. Stress can lead to chronic pain, frequent sickness, insomnia, digestive issues, depression, nervousness, rapid heartbeat and sweating.

Yes, sweating! It was one week before that fateful day, 3 July 2012, on my return from our lawyers that my wife was concerned about my sweating profusely in our taxi home. If I had only known that these beads of sweat were a sign of my impending stroke, I would have gone to the hospital. Waking up in a cold sweat, feeling nauseated, and vomiting may be symptoms of the flu, but they can also be signs of a cardiovascular attack. The ominous cold beads of sweat were indeed a sign.

'Cold sweats' refers to sudden sweating that doesn't come from heat or exertion. The medical term for cold sweats is 'diaphoresis'. It comes from the body's response to stress, called the fight-or-flight response. The fight-or-flight response, which helped ancient humans survive in a more physically dangerous world, prepared the body to battle with an enemy or run away.

How much of our stress is determined by our mindset? Well, I thought I was fine, and then I suffered a stroke! Personal experience tells me that stress has insidious stealth capabilities; it will sneak up on you because few of us are focused on what our heart is telling us. Instead, we are focused on spreadsheets, sales, customer service, success, and the next big deal. On the weekends, we focus on family, shopping, sports, errands, and getting ready for Monday. We are in our heads, but we need to be in our hearts.

I began to shift to researching stress, more so to contain and beat it.

Believe it or not, some stress is good. In fact, we need a certain kind of stress to survive, and it's called eustress (contrast this with negative stress or distress, the kind that is mostly referred to). Eustress could be the result of a challenging work assignment that is neither too difficult nor too easy. This stress motivates in the short term, feels good, and improves performance.

The next kind of stress is physical stress that comes in the form of physical exercise, which is important for our health. However, if the body is subjected to too much physical stress, as with overtraining, it will increase the acids in our body, accelerate ageing, and cause cell degeneration. I will always remember that moderation is key.

I realised a lot later that a heart rate variability constantly stressed by a challenged state intertwined with an unhealthy lifestyle could lead to a low vagal tone. In 2021, I heard of this rather interesting finding. This totally gave me a sense of control in how stress could invade my body. If only I had known this, I would have taken more steps to increase my vagal tone and manage my stress better.

My Blueprint for Stress Management: In Pursuit of a Healthy Vagal Tone

My illness gave me time to reflect on where I was going wrong. Regarding stroke prevention, if only I had known the importance of focusing on having a healthy and strong vagal tone, I may have indeed prevented my stroke.

If you want to change your life, you have to find different ways of doing things. Setting an intent without following up with action doesn't work. To turn a dream into reality, thought needs to combine with physical action. One of my favourite anonymous quotes sums this up: 'If you always do what you have always done, you will always get what you have always got.'

My ardent wish for all who are chasing dreams is to live that life of intent and remember your dream plans do come with hidden, potential write-offs. By this, I mean the sacrifices and compromises we make of our health to fulfil that dream at the expense of all other equally important aspects of our life. We can indeed prevent the onset of stroke and many debilitating illnesses by just doing that.

Once I had my stroke, I had to maintain a strong sense of conviction, particularly as I was recovering from a serious internal meltdown. To get better results, we must change the input. My book aims to bring different concepts to you so that you can benefit through my experience. You must never give up all efforts in your recovery process no matter how many inner challenges you face.

Sleep: Ferrari Mind, Fiat Body

I wasn't sleeping well six months before my stroke. That got worse the days before my stroke when I was sleeping very little. I was headed toward a frightening disaster, but my focus was elsewhere. I was worried about the $4.5 million I owed to my partners and wouldn't be able to pay on time. The financial burden was too much for me, and I underestimated the stress this would cause. I thought I could cope, but my body answered with a resounding 'no'. I call this *Ferrari mind, Fiat body*.

Current thinking suggests that the mind is all powerful, but I discovered that the body must be able to keep up with your thoughts. If it can't, it creates imbalance, and in time, something will give. I had created so much pressure that my mind and body were looking for a release valve. They found it in an artery, and I am extremely fortunate to have survived and to have defied even the doctors' expectations with my recovery.

I may not have noticed the warning signs, but my wife sees it differently. She told me that before my stroke, I often lost my train of thought, became more forgetful, and unexpectedly broke out in cold sweats. If you or your partner suspect something might be wrong, please get a simple blood pressure test, check your resting heart rate, and work with a general practitioner. It's better to be overly cautious than to not pay attention, and if you ignore your suspicions and something is wrong, there's a brick wall ahead waiting for you to smash into it.

Monitoring Your Health as a Lifestyle: Mind over Body

My stroke cost me millions of dollars in actual and potential revenue while also causing a great deal of physical pain and sadness that I would not wish on anyone. What could I have done differently to relieve the stress that built up during the six months prior to my stroke? Now that I know how destructive stress can be, if I could rewind the clock, I would make every effort to acknowledge and address the sources of my stress.

I know not to make the same mistakes again. I sleep better now that I have learned to be more measured and to consider all factors before making major decisions. Understanding how to master my mind, so that I don't slip into unconscious modes, helps me to relax and breathe my way through work and life, rather than allowing my body to turn against itself as the stress response is activated.

If you have trouble sleeping, there is a simple visualisation technique that can help. At night, focus on your breath, in through the nose and out through the nose. You can visualise the earth and everyone living on it melting away. This technique is called 'nothingness'. By the time you wake in the morning and your feet first touch the floor after getting out of bed, the earth has magically recreated itself. It's a fresh start.

Some of the lifestyle changes that might be beneficial are not to take more than you can handle and to keep your debt level and workload manageable. Have a pressure release valve in the form of sport, meditation, yoga, fun with friends, or a walk to the local park along with exercise several times a week, as well as regular massages or spa treatments.

Having a mentor or good friend who has experience in whatever you are about to undertake is a great way to reduce stress, as educated debate helps to clearly outline all the scenarios. Perhaps the person you are discussing the subject with has the experience to offer solutions that you haven't thought of or will ask you key questions. Two heads are better than one. These strategies can save you time, money, pain and suffering. It feels good to get things off your chest. Don't bottle things up, as this is not good for you. Work at having good relations with all your contacts.

Earthing: A Totally New Concept to Me

Another concept to consider is 'earthing'. Earthing was discovered and introduced to the world by Clinton Ober, Dr. Stephen Sinatra, and Martin Zucker. It is simple: Take your shoes off and walk around on the grass for 20 or 30 minutes barefoot. Your body will automatically dump the radiation from your cell phone, computer, and work environment that has accumulated in your cells. Earthing should be done every day to restore balance and healing and to relieve built-up stress in the mind and body. This originates from the Native Americans. A good read on this is *Down to Earth*.

Breathwork: Do It Right!

While earthing, focus on breathing to reduce stress. Open your lungs to reoxygenate your body. There are many great breathing techniques that produce fantastic results. Most of us are not very good at breathing, yet it is fundamental to survival. We can last without food for 30 days and without water for seven, but without oxygen, we are dead in minutes.

The heart is one of the first places affected by stress in the body. Our breathing patterns determine how fast our heart beats. If you start running, it is natural for the pulse to increase so as to quickly remove carbon dioxide and lactic acid. This is a way for the body to avoid becoming toxic. My resting heart rate was about 90 beats per minute when I had my stroke— much too fast! Now it's under 70. By doing meditation, my goal is to get down to 60 beats per minute within a year. By then, my heart rate will be lower than my age.

I use meditation to better control my breathing and heart rate. If I can get my heart to 60 beats per minute, and curb my excessive thinking, then more energy can be used for my body's internal healing processes. The brain uses an average of 20 percent of the body's energy, yet it makes up only 7 percent of the body's weight. If you think a lot, then the burning of glucose to fuel your mind could be as high as 30 percent.[17]

With meditation, the mind becomes trained to think and focus. It is not about stopping all thoughts. Meditation is also nonsectarian and nonreligious. It is pure energy. Meditation reduces the heart rate, removes mental clutter, releases relaxing hormones from pineal and pituitary glands, reduces thought, and creates inner peace, stillness, and calm.

Meditation: Mind over Matter

So, how can we effectively relieve stress? One of the best ways I have found is through meditation. Meditation is simply an exercise, a mode, or a state, like sleep or being awake. Once trained, you can easily shift your mind to this zone. It does take a little practice, but it is a very natural thing to do. Here's why: science says when you go from being awake to asleep, your brainwaves shift from beta (12–40 Hz) to alpha (8–12 Hz) and eventually to theta (4–8 Hz).[18] This is the normal process when the brain winds down.

There is a very good reason for this. Our brain cycles down from what's called a waking state to resonate with the pulse of the earth. This pulse is 7.83 Hz. This heartbeat or magnetic field is called the Schuman resonance and was identified by a German scientist of the same name.

When we go to sleep, our brains automatically slow down and sync up with the magnetic field of the earth, just like an iPhone syncs with a computer. The same thing happens when you meditate, except that the process is faster than when you are asleep. Instead of taking a few hours, someone who is trained in meditation can shift the mind from beta waves to alpha waves to theta waves and then to delta waves all in a few minutes. That makes meditation an advanced form of sleep that produces greater restorative results.

When faced with a health challenge, meditating to reduce your thoughts is very helpful. It frees up energy used by your brain that can be directed to other areas. If you are healthy, and you reduce your thoughts, the energy saved can be used for the maintenance of good health, helping others, and even sports.

Meditation has also proven to regenerate your cells and boost your immune system. CEOs and celebrities use meditation to help with their health and to become more confident and dynamic. Among those who have benefited from meditation are Sir Richard Branson, Jerry Seinfeld, Hugh Jackman, Nicole Kidman, Oprah Winfrey, Jeff Weiner, Arianna Huffington, and Padmasree Warrior.

Inner Power X: Fire Breath or Kapal Bhati

In addition to meditation, one of the first things I do every day is a pro-gramme called Inner Power X, or IPX. IPX can be done by anyone. It is the ancient art of increasing your personal energy and health by performing a specifically designed set of gentle breathing and physical exercises. The techniques are a combination of tai chi, chi kung, and yoga, and they can easily be modified to suit any age and fitness level. The IPX programme originates from Tamil Nadu, a state in India.

IPX will enhance, repair, and detox your physical body at an accelerated rate, increase your energy, and protect, enrich, and deliver much-needed vital force to help you better cope with the increasing stress of modern life.

The instructor, Raja Mohan, who does treatments for me, coaches elderly people at the Ang Mo Kio Community Centre in Singapore. IPX makes a big difference almost instantly. They look, feel, and act much more energetic after the class.

With IPX, the breath is called 'fire breath.' In Sanskrit it is called *kapalbhati*. In just a few minutes of breathing, your cheeks will be rosy, you will be less stressed, and your body will be highly oxygenated. And this will give you a large energy boost. It can be done twice a day, prior to eating, but the instructors caution against performing the exercise after the sun sets because you want to give your body enough time to wind down.

Inner Power X consists of a set of six exercises. They can best be described as gentle but dynamic yoga poses that bend and twist the body in a relaxed and safe way. They make the body stronger and more flexible, particularly in the legs and lower energy centres. Because of my stroke, I do a modified version, but I can feel that it has made me more resilient. I'm looking forward to tackling the complete set soon.

Yoga: A System of Living

Yoga is another great activity for the mind, body, and spirit. I have recently used partner yoga to accelerate my recovery, enhance my motor skills, and increase the neuroplasticity of my brain, while the breathing exercises boosted my immune system and stimulated regeneration.

I do a custom class adapted to suit my rehabilitation needs. And if *I* can do it, anyone can. The trick is to pick the right instructor who listens to your needs and understands your body. My instructor helps take my legs and arms to places where they otherwise wouldn't be able to move.

Yoga is much more than just exercise—that is just one aspect. Yoga is actually a complex and heightened system of living. The other aspects are healing, mind training, eating, breathing, vegetarianism, and spirituality. Energy should also be included, but outside India, very little is known or even discussed about the energetic aspects of yoga. The chakras play a large part in the function of the central nervous system. The more blocked the meridians and chakras, the lower the function of the central nervous system and a person's mobility. Yoga helps to unblock the energy centres in our bodies.

If you have an illness or are recovering from a meltdown, whether it is physical or mental, yoga is definitely one of the essential things you should include in your recovery regime. Start with the easy poses and build from there.

Whether we do meditation, yoga, or exercise, the ancillary benefit is that it helps keep our mind in the present. 'Try to live in the present moment,' Eckhart Tolle wrote in his book, *The Power of Now*, which is recommended by Oprah Winfrey.[19]

Typically, we generate stress when our minds are stuck in the past or the future because it takes us away from what's happening now. When we try to relive moments that we can never get back again, we beat ourselves up over it. Then the cycle repeats itself. Those what-if scenarios can produce a lot of heavy mental clutter.

Positive Self-Talk: A Self-Awareness Exercise

When I find my mood being affected by negative self-talk, I quickly reset and focus on lighter, brighter, happier moments. It's not that the dark thoughts have been suppressed; it's that I have learned to just observe them. I've learned that I don't need to judge them or react to them. It's an exercise in self-awareness. Observe the thoughts you normally consider draining, but do not judge or react to them. Then focus on those thoughts that make you come alive and give you energy. It's a simple exercise.

Focusing on the current moment allows you to release tension in the body and diffuse emotional anxiety. Try to find words that put situations in a positive light but still allow you to stay true to yourself. Choose to say 'maybe' instead of 'no' when appropriate. Choose encouragement, enthusiasm, and passion as fuel to fire up your dreams and the hopes of others.

A positive way to reduce stress and fear in your life is to view yourself as not needing to be attached to or detached from ideas, people, or things. You learn to see that you have the power of choice and that you are fully in control of how you participate in whatever is in front of you. Go through your processes at work or on the home front, and then try to let go of the result. If you have done your best and can't do anymore, then there's nothing further to do; close the chapter, and move on to the next thing you want to get done.

Letting Go: A Culture of Control

The world is far too wound up these days, and we all need to experience a safe environment outside the 'culture of control' to learn to trust ourselves and trust that our needs will be met. As long as we do our part, the universe will deliver a fair and ultimately positive outcome for all concerned. Make letting go a central exercise, and you will have less stress. You will be surprised by the additional rewards.

If your desire doesn't manifest as you had planned, then perhaps there is something better around the corner. So don't despair, and stay present so you don't miss it when it comes. Go with it, be patient, and look forward to new discoveries and adventures. One day, you and I will no longer be around, so sooner or later we will have to start trusting that the world will be fine on its own. We can never stop learning, and in 2019, I discovered two devices that could help me let go and feel safe. This is when I was introduced to the concepts of Heart Math and the Low Energy Neurofeedback System therapy (LENS).

Heart Math

This involves using a device called Inner Balance. When I started using it in April 2019, I found that I was able to quiet my mind, and this created peace and tranquillity during the session. It allowed me to sleep better, and it also allowed me to meditate better.

LENS Therapy

In April 2019, I found a centre that was able to do a neurofeedback session with me that was different from that of other centres. Psychologist Lee Chan was trained in the United States by Dr. Ochs. As I went through the twice weekly sessions, I found that I was less emotional, and I realised that this would be key to my continued recovery. LENS was developed by Len Ochs, PhD, a northern-California psychologist. LENS was created as an alternative to medication for brain-based problems and is often used along with psychotherapy. LENS directly stimulates biochemical changes that are thought to help the brain regulate itself.

The treatment uses tiny electrodes affixed to the scalp with conductive paste to both measure the brainwave activity and to deliver treatment. It is completely painless and noninvasive. It is effective because the brain can respond to a low-energy signal, whereas it would react and defend against a stronger one. I felt better after doing this treatment. I found out that LENS would make the brain more flexible, and the therapy provides the support and coaching for how to make changes and develop new patterns in how we deal with our thoughts and emotions.

Nature's Frequencies

In 2020, I started using Nature's Frequencies patches. My favourite is the Sleep Patch, which uses Biofield Resonance Technology™, to help me with deeper sleep. The Sleep Patch is designed to help calm the mind and body so you can get the deep resonance sleep you need.

A Winning Formula for Stroke Recovery

There is no magic bullet or quick fix, but I have developed a winning formula for recovery from paralysis caused by a stroke:

Neuroplasticity + Hard work + Time + Faith = Recovery.

Stated another way: Neuroplasticity is the foundation of stroke recovery. It's how your brain rewires itself after injury, with the process being initiated by repetitive movement.

You don't need to physically make the movements yourself to initiate neuroplasticity; assisted movement and mental movement also count. Self-belief also plays a big part. If you have an iron will and are focused on maximising your recovery, you stand a better chance of regaining your function. That is not to say that simply wishing yourself well will produce a miraculous result; you need to put in the hard work, be positive, and truly believe you can exceed expectations.

<u>Now let the miracles begin!</u>

CHAPTER 17

THE POWER OF MOVEMENT

The doctor of the future will give no medicine but will involve the patient in the proper use of food, fresh air, and exercise.

—Thomas Edison[20]

I have never been sporty or athletic. After being bullied at the age of 15, I purchased a Bullworker that had just entered the market and that revolutionised the process of exercising for muscle strength. After training myself on the Bullworker for six months, I started to develop six-pack abs, and I wasn't bullied any more.

Driven by my mission, which was to excel in my academics, my sole preoccupation during my university days was my studies. Only during my days at the Brunel University London did I begin to enjoy tennis. Then, in 1991, I felt the need to build my inner strength, and I took up an ancient form of martial arts, Nam Wah Pai, for two years.

Motivation struck me again in 2002 to train twice a week for three months to do a 700 km cyclothon with 30 other cyclists from Ipoh to Singapore, over four days, to raise funds for the Sikh Welfare Society. However, my daily routine soon became too busy for me to even consider infusing exercise into my life. Ironically, I only began exercise again because of stress and lack of sleep.

In October 2018, I was inspired to buy another Bullworker to rebuild my atrophied muscles and my confidence, 47 years after I had achieved such great results from it the first time around. Since my stroke, I've exercised more than I ever have in my life.

Riding for Charity, 2002

Exercising with my Bull Worker in 2021

Today, I am fully engaged and driven toward achieving mobility, but I face new challenges that begin every morning when I wake up in my half-paralysed body. As I sleep, I have to position my right arm in the direction I wish to face, but that continually disrupts my sleep throughout the night. There is a heaviness in my legs that often makes movement difficult throughout the day, but I know that the faster I can get my body back to its automated state, the quicker I will become independent and not have to rely on others for support. That motivates me to exercise.

Back in 2003, the BioResonance System (BRS), designed during the Russian space programme to help cosmonauts maintain healthy frequencies in space, was first introduced into Atos Wellness. Since then, I have used BRS as a lifestyle therapy, and I am happy with its results. Both before and after the stroke, this therapeutic mat has often brought me relief. And now my company has invested in a device called the WHT Energy Mat.

Atos WHT Energy Mat

Bio-Resonance Mat in 2008

From 2012 to 2020, I experienced several healing protocols, including traditional and contemporary therapies. These come from various countries, and all are intended to achieve the same common goal: bringing my body into balance.

It was only when I met Vincent Yong in 2018 that I saw the power of movement at one of the SNSA activities. I was intrigued by this young man who spoke with such passion on the need to create rapport through movement in the same shared space between the caregiver and the stroke survivor. This is about turning inward to understand the inner world and its connection with the outer world through our bodies. Breathing helps one experience one's body and life, and their presence and existence. As patients become more aware of their own life support, they begin to tap into that sense of gratitude as they start to appreciate their other senses.

Vincent explained clearly that movement creates an avenue for the stroke survivor to become confident of their movements through their ability to engage and activate their bodies for better balance. It is only if a stroke survivor expresses his reaffirmation of his achievement and confidence in his own action and movement that he will be able to assimilate and apply all the information he gains from his senses. Dance supports the health of individuals through many aspects of muscular coordination and endurance through repetition and refinement of movement sequences. Balance, stamina, strength, flexibility and fitness are all by-products of practice. Dance also improves memory, both cognitive as well as muscular.

Since I had my stroke, I've had physiotherapists monitor my progress and provide me with a range of exercise protocols, including the Berg Balance Scale, which indicates the risk assessment of suffering a fall. There is still room for me to improve, but my progress from 2015 to 2018 showed that I had moved from 45/56 to 50/56.

My daily walks in 2014

My daily walks in 2018

Exercising with my physiotherapist

Exercising on the Treadmill with the Spinoflex in 2021

Both the muscle power and range of motion assessments were done periodically to show how much I had progressed during the series of exercises. The physiotherapists also designed a series of treatment protocols consisting of upper limb exercises, lower limb exercises, bar exercises, bed exercises, Vivafit stepper, multifunction exercises, and Bioresonance sessions. Meanwhile, my caregivers were trained to aid with yoga stretches, Varma Kalai follow-up exercise and stretch routines, daily walks, and vibration training. Other treatments and exercise protocols were provided by my various therapists including Dada A. Ananyananda, M. Segar, Greg Watters, Raja Mohan, and Kulbhushan Kakar.

My exercise routine in 2021

Yoga & Meditation with Dada Ananyananda in 2019

These exercises helped provide constant motivation because every measure of improvement brought me one step closer to regaining my mobility and strength in my still-paralysed right side. I have collated all the findings in my progress reports, which I have included in the appendix section 4 on page 187. I have also included all the protocols that I performed, and you can see how much effort I painstakingly put in during my never-ending drive to return to a state as close to normality as humanly possible. I am frequently reminded about how much I have improved by those who have not seen me in a long time and are able to recognise the great progress I have made. It gives me so much joy and satisfaction to know that I am moving in the right direction.

CHAPTER 18

PLANNING FOR THE FUTURE

Every minute you spend in planning saves 10 minutes in execution; this gives you a 1,000 percent return on energy!

—Brian Tracy[21]

Over the last nine years, it has been difficult for me to accept that new image of myself at work. And it must also have been difficult for others to accept me in this new vulnerable state.

My steady progress keeps me energised. And while exploring business opportunities, I have also renewed my passion to serve humanity.

During my recovery, I have been mindful not to fall into complacency, so in between my treatments, I devour books and attend workshops to keep abreast of developments within the wellness industry. I have also begun to look at various business models that would allow me to build a passive income stream once this book is launched. This income is to fund my various charities that help people in need.

Renewed with my regained passion, I began to evaluate the various options that avail to one like me. My life after the stroke drove me to research further into the world of those who have been inflicted by this debilitating condition. In Singapore, some statistics show 8,000 people a year suffer from a stroke.[22] And if you factor in that many of us live for 10 to 20 years after the stroke, we could have more than 80,000 people. And that's just in

Singapore! What options indeed lie ahead of us? This search led me closer toward the world of affiliate marketing.

Affiliate Marketing: An Empowering Business Opportunity

If you look at developed societies around the world, you will see that we are already in the early stages of moving away from the traditional pay-per-hour scheme. Our collective wants and needs are shifting because our own attitudes toward life and work have shifted. It may have been said that my father lived during uncertain times, but ironically, today's times are no less uncertain. While much of the world has changed, that is the one thing that has stayed the same.

In this climate, the affiliate marketing (network marketing) model has begun to seem much more appealing. Businesses in the wellness sector can offer consumers simple solutions for achieving what they crave most—an independent and relatively unburdened life. When you look at businesses that are on the rise, you can clearly see that the wellness industry is doing well. One simply needs to move in tandem with the times.

Having studied the direct-selling model for the last five years, I saw the huge potential it offered. The book *Rich Dad, Poor Dad* by Robert Kiyosaki provided me with some interesting theories that I was eager to put to the test after being able to restore my health to a certain level by 2014. Kiyosaki describes a business model called network marketing and why he feels it could be good for the 21st century. As he observes, the perceptions people have about wealth play a huge role in the nature of the money they make. While wealth is often perceived to be the money we accumulate in proportion to the effort we put in, Kiyosaki defined wealth in terms of *how long* one's money would continue flowing even *after* they stopped working. I was intrigued.

This method is more comparable to earning rewards every time you recommend to a friend a great product that you're using. Although I was not unfamiliar with these ideas, they truly began to make more sense after my stroke. I liked how Kiyosaki encouraged readers to rethink their method of making money and how toiling away to earn income does not necessarily help to create long-term wealth. Instead, people can take control of their financial lives by working to seed a stream of passive income. And that passive income will continue to flow even after the initial financial and time commitment. As for me, I wanted there to be a focus on good products that sell themselves, as well as real relationships that bring the community together and don't alienate anyone.

Reflecting on what I had learned so far, I saw that the affiliate business approach could be the key to what I could do in the future. This is especially true for the millions of people around the world who, like me, cannot get ordinary work due to paralysis or other serious illness. Robert Kiyosaki's *Rich Dad, Poor Dad* showed me that there were options I could create for myself, so that my earning potential could increase even without my hourly effort. The key was to allow a shift in my mindset regarding wealth and income generation. I had made many contacts over the years, and I could turn to them when the time was right. Any of the millions of people worldwide who are recovering from a stroke or other debilitating diseases could do the same thing with their network. And this would also be true for families, retirees, and stay-at-home parents who desire more income.

Vivafit: A New Business Plan

In March 2016, I read an article in the newspapers about a ladies' fitness franchise called Vivafit that was closing four locations. It reminded me of the days when I made it my business to rescue spas. My heart went out to them.

Prior to reading the article, I had been approached by a couple who were the owners of its subfranchise. They asked me for help in running their two locations in Beach Road and Bukit Merah after not turning a profit in three years. Curiously, Vivafit was already doing well overseas and was represented in more than 10 other countries.

I contacted the outgoing master franchisor, Jonas Orgen, who was able to provide the contacts of their 1,000 members, whom we contacted and then arranged for alternative gym memberships, yoga or spa treatments.

The big question was how we could make Vivafit profitable again. The topic of women's fitness sparked my interest as I saw that it was synergistic with our wellness business. In July 2016, the couple decided to close their businesses and approached me to take over their two operations. Since I believed Vivafit to be a complement to our wellness business, Atos Wellness bought the master franchise in August 2016.

Those recent developments with Atos Wellness and Vivafit renewed my zest for business again. I felt that this provided me with a new lease on life by creating a new direction for Atos Wellness. Like Papa, who had worked at his business up to the age of 72, I felt that I was healthy enough to create a successful business. The rescue instinct within me rekindled the rush of adrenalin I had always felt when I rescued many a spa.

We took over the Vivafit centre in Bukit Merah. I felt that the concept lacked a nutrition component, which I was also keen to explore. However, my enthusiasm was short lived since we were new to the fitness world, and the sudden Vivafit closures made it impossible to rekindle the Vivafit brand. So, I decided to hold back on our master franchise plan until later. Shortly after Vivafit's closure of the previous master franchise centres in 2016, California Fitness closed its 20-year-old chain of fitness centres in Singapore. That was a blow, but there is always hope.

While the world keeps changing, there are some things that do not change. For one, the key to opening all doors remains the same, and that is creating a successful business plan. I'm simply waiting for the right time to reopen the Vivafit franchise with a suitable nutrition product.

Life after Stroke

Back to work with elevated confidence with Trish Schwenkler, a Triple Presidential Diamond

After the stroke, I was haunted by the thought that I might not be as financially independent as I was before, but studying Kiyosaki's concepts allowed me to understand some of the ways I could break out on that road to financial independence, and I soon found success with a company called ASEA.

I started to take ASEA in January 2018, and with the help of my team, I was able to build a small business by 2021 that allowed me to earn an average income of $3,000 a month. This has elevated my confidence, and now I want to share this with other stroke survivors.

As I continued with my treatments, I also realised that many people who had similar issues could not afford the same treatments, especially those underinsured. Some Singaporeans hold two jobs because it is what they need to do to survive. To make ends meet, many work longer hours, yet with longer life expectancies, many fear not having enough retirement savings.

Illness can come suddenly and with devastating results, just as it did in my case. I was incredibly fortunate to have my own business and also a wife to run my company. What would have happened to me if I had been a regular, salaried employee? My employer would not have kept me around for more than two months! And if I hadn't had insurance, I would have been left with a crippling medical debt. How could someone get out of that predicament?

That's when I knew that it would be important for me to test this concept of affiliate marketing because its principles are about *teaching people how to fish* rather than *giving them a fish*. It lets people subsidise their own consumption by successfully sharing what they already buy and like. The bar of entry is low, which means that you don't need to have a business or sales background but simply share how the product helped you.

What you need is the right attitude, mainly to be self-motivated and to think like an entrepreneur. Even taxi and Grab drivers, who often speak of their own difficulty in covering their costs, can benefit from this kind of business model in their free time. I wanted to use these theories, together with my knowledge and expertise in traditional business, to help people along on their journeys.

SNSA Stroke Advocate

Opportunities abound when there is an attraction of wills. In one of these SNSA programmes, I met Vincent Yong, who had just completed a dance session for stroke survivors. Vincent found me approachable and appreciative of his efforts that day. Vincent shared in one of my meetings with him that he saw my fight against my condition with the spirit of openness and a keen sense of learning.

As I shared with him the various avenues of the healing journey I had undertaken over the years, Vincent felt that I was seeking a transcendence, something that would lift me above the situation and tie me to something bigger. I felt he empathised with my desire to be truly understood—the real Aanandha within me. I felt comforted that Vincent could feel the real struggle within me, and he was aligned with what I felt: dance as a form of therapy or healing can only happen with empathy for the physical, mental, and emotional resonance within ourselves.

Since I had difficulty expressing myself, Vincent said this of me, and I share: 'I knew Aanandha's search for healing was more than just regaining normal function such as the traditional practice of physiotherapy I have seen at hospitals. He wanted something more holistic. Aanandha was looking for something that could communicate deeply with him—body, mind, and soul.'[23]

This I found so profoundly spot-on that I saw this form of dance—as movement therapy or education—as a wonderful collaboration. Vincent could possibly expand the modes of access to fitness and wellness so more stroke survivors could benefit from this. These thoughts inspired me further to seek ways and means to engage the many minds now shackled by stroke. These in actuality seemed to drive my spirit to break out and boost my body toward recovery as I moved in the direction of my newly found mission—to serve society beyond my physical limitations.

Strangely, at this juncture of tragedy and a burning desire, I now fully embraced the change that had suddenly struck me in 2012. Once I fully embraced the change , I developed a desire to become a stroke advocate for the Singapore National Stroke Association (SNSA) so I could help people develop a better understanding of how to manage life after a stroke. I first joined SNSA in 2015, and I found that its programmes were very beneficial to me as they allowed me to be part of a community of like-minded persons who had experienced stroke. In 2019, I was voted on the executive committee and served for two years.

Elected as SNSA Executive Committee in 2020

Activities at SNSA

Writing My Story

That's not the only thing that I have set my sights on. After my encounter with Dr. Darren Weissman, I developed another plan for the future: writing a book that documented my story and my stroke-recovery journey. When I had my stroke, the awakening realities became so onerous, and now I felt compelled to do something to help guide others who were stuck in a similar state. The lessons I have learned from my experience of these past nine years have left me with a burning desire to spread the word about how to overcome tragedy in order to experience gratitude, truth, happiness and healing.

I have documented in my book what I personally have gone through and found useful in my journey to recovery. It serves as a resource guide for stroke survivors when they embark on their own journeys to wellness. Nevertheless, I advise everyone to speak with their doctors if they have any health concerns before they go about these journeys.

The New Normal World: Yet Another Tumultuous Journey

One thing COVID-19 has taught us is how we do not need to go into an office to work or do business. The world's GDP seems to be pretty good with people doing their business from home. Not optimal, but pretty good.

Accordingly, as people in many cases coped quite easily with working from home, you, too, might be surprised by how you can adapt without all the mobility you enjoyed before. Be positive about how you might use your knowledge and skills in your new situation. As I have frequently encountered in my life, you will encounter roadblocks. What is most important is to try not to be disheartened. Perseverance is the key. Adapt as you go. Think of new ideas. Keep going.

One of the sobering aspects in my early days of stroke recovery is confronting my own financial position. These thoughts constantly arise in me: you must evaluate what your financial position is after the stroke, taking into account treatment costs, how much money you need, what assets you have, and what capability you have in generating an income.

It makes sense to have a trusted financial adviser. It makes even more sense for you to understand whatever assets you have and how they might be invested going forward. Many people find accounting, financial forms, and investing too dry. You should take an active interest and increase your knowledge of what investments you have, how are they performing, and what management fees are you paying. If you haven't taken any interest before, now is an opportunity to use your time and attention on this area of core importance in your life.

I would expect that many people who make the effort to understand investment options can quickly learn that this can indeed be a fascinating area. Here is where you need to plan out your wealth creation and financial position and also do retirement planning. Part of taking control of your life is being in control of your financial affairs, whether you have modest means or are well off.

Part of the next level of thinking and planning is considering to what extent you might invest. There is, in fact, a huge variety of investment options including investment funds, hedge funds, and derivatives. You don't really need to delve into sophisticated financial instruments. Make sure you cover the basics.

It is beyond the scope of this book to provide you with an investment template. But the point is to make sure you understand your financial position. Learn more about your investment options, take an interest in financial markets, keep your assets diversified, and do your best to understand how much you can aim for growing your assets versus your need for income stability.

It is wise to get plenty of good advice. Good financial planning should include an element of being charitable and giving back to society. These will ensure that we stand on solid ground when we plan for our future. Thankfully for me, this is not new. I have always believed in setting aside my time and resources to help those who were less endowed in life when they were struck down in life—all the more reason we must step up in this area of giving. The joys of giving can never be understated. Give more to receive more. Giving without any expectation of receiving anything in return is even better.

CHAPTER 19

GIVING BACK TO SOCIETY

*As you grow older, you will discover that you have two hands—one for
helping yourself, the other for helping others.*

–Audrey Hepburn

As I pushed forward with total dedication toward my rehabilitation,
it dawned on me that I was restless inside. Something seemed to be
missing in my life. It was only when I started meditating again that I was
struck by a feeling that I had first experienced back in 1995. It was déjà vu.

In 1995, I was stuck at a numbing crossroad in life. I had a failing
business and a young family that depended on me. While meditating
at the ashram in Puttaparthi, I was made painfully aware of the core
purpose that had driven me at age 17 and then again when I interned at
British Petroleum in 1980. That inner call to serve humanity sounded
from the deep recesses of my mind. I was struck with the sense of purpose
again in 1995, and I felt rejuvenated. It was like new life was surging
through my veins. I returned to Singapore with renewed vigour and spirit to succeed, driven by that deep inner call to serve beyond myself and
my existence. I reflected, and I promised to stay true to that conviction
to serve humanity *without* getting dragged into the humdrum of business
and its ups and downs.

Charitable Projects

As I discussed my plans with Manjit, who had encouraged me to go to Put-taparthi, I decided to join him in many charitable causes to start my journey to serve with immediacy and the commitment of my time and resources. Many causes came my way, and I wholeheartedly engaged in them.

My journey began with my weekly trips to St Joseph's Home, which I had first visited in 1995 when I was introduced to Sister Geraldine. Man-jit and I decided to visit St Joseph's Home on Saturday mornings with a tasty range of breakfast treats that delighted our newly found friends at the home. We bought local savouries like *epok-epok, nasi lemak, ham chim peng, chee cheong fun, thosai,* and *roti prata* and also sweet delights like rainbow *kueh-kueh* and *putu-mayam*. It wasn't long before my young family also joined me on Saturdays, and that ritual continued for the next 16 years, only to end abruptly after that fateful Tuesday in July of 2012.

That was not my only endeavour that came to a stop after my stroke. I had supported and championed many causes, regardless of race, language, or religion, as long as they brought happiness and solace to those who had been left out by society.

Baan Unrak in 2005

Sister Didi and the Ananda Marga Society ran an orphanage called Baan Unrak (House of Joy) for stateless children caught up in the conflict at the Thailand–Myanmar border. Manjit introduced me to Sister Didi in 2010, and I supported them by volunteering my time and by funding projects for the school. We supported orphaned boys in India through the Ananda Marga Society. That nourished the desire within me to serve more humanitarian causes. Part of the reason that I was able to endure that 700 km charity bike ride from Ipoh to Singapore, even though I didn't exercise regularly, was my drive to make a difference.

More opportunities came my way when a friend approached me to seek funding for a Buddhist cause. Although I was born a Hindu, I felt comfortable, and I went ahead and supported that cause without question.

 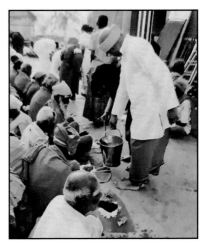

Brahmarishi Hills in Tamilnadu in 2011

Another calling came in 2011 from the Brahmarishi Hills. There, I served by feeding the many hungry families that came to the hills for solace and support. Pathma and I went up and said prayers at the top of the Brahmarishi Hills where holy men and siddhas gathered periodically to mingle with society again, taking time away from self-imposed solitude and meditation.

Then in 2016, while meditating, I was suddenly jolted, and I reflected on my current state. I felt once again disabled by my stroke, in the same way that

I had been stuck in my busy business problems and the desire to grow bigger and bigger prior to my stroke. I was so consumed with getting back to my former self that I had once again forgotten the need to serve. I realised that I could do both. I could focus on my own health challenges while helping people get over their difficulties. I didn't need to wait until I was completely better.

That familiar call to serve surged through my half-paralysed body. *Am I going to be defined by my current physical state, or am I going to go beyond and strike out to give back to society once again?* I knew that I was still able to do that. I was not disabled by what had happened to me. And I became humbled by the fact that I could still do it. It was while feeling that renewed energy in 2016 that another opportunity to participate in a charity bike race came up, this one to raise funds for World Vision and Society for Wings. Despite my physical limitations, I signed up without hesitation, as it was a stationary bike event.

Renewed Energy at a spin bike charity event, 2016

Back to Riding for Charity

I have documented the many experiences I went through before and after my stroke. I have met so many people through many journeys to bring my body back into balance. I have come across a range of modalities from the best of both the East and the West, while actively trying to better understand why this happened to me. Now, giving back to society has come to motivate me to further overcome my current obstacles and to help those facing similar challenges or feeling out of sync with society.

After my book is published, I intend to focus on another organisation, Doctors Without Borders (DWB). This organisation was started in France more than 40 years ago as a way for doctors to make a difference in countries that have been torn apart by strife and war. When I was 17, I wanted to be a doctor and go to a developing country, and now I hope this book will do well so the proceeds can help their cause as well as other charitable organisations.

I greatly benefited from the Singapore National Stroke Association (SNSA). SNSA is part of the regional and international stroke community and is a member of the Asia Pacific Stroke Organisation (APSO) and the World Stroke Organization. In 2019 these were just some of the programmes and activities, organised by SNSA, that I and 2,026 other stroke survivors have benefited from at no cost because we are members.[24]

SNSA has three key missions: (1) to *support* stroke survivors and caregivers; (2) to raise stroke *awareness* by educating the public, stroke survivors, and their families; and (3) to serve as an *advocate* for the stroke community.

Stroke survivors like myself were engaged in activities organised by a driven team of volunteers and SNSA staff. I thoroughly enjoyed the L.I.F.E. sessions (Learn, Integrate, Flourish, and Engage) that I used to attend twice a month. The objective of these sessions was to create opportunities for survivors to relearn to integrate effectively back into society in a meaningful and enriching way. Our SNSA activities included diverse activities like mindfulness sessions and music and art therapies, to name a few.

I particularly looked forward to our social gatherings and evening strolls around Singapore. The one I most vividly remember is the one at the Stadium Walk. We also had our exercise during sports activities like table tennis, lawn bowling, and even seated tai chi. Befriending events held at the six SNSA-participating hospitals were created to infuse engaging activities in a fun-filled setting where like-minded personnel meet and interact with those with similar shared experiences.

In November 2018, SNSA launched a new programme called 'Chit Chat Café' to specifically cater to stroke survivors suffering from aphasia, which affects about 25–30 percent of stroke survivors.[25] A stroke causes permanent damage in the brain resulting in neurological deficits, and aphasia is one of these deficits. Those suffering from aphasia have difficulty understanding and expressing themselves verbally and through writing. I didn't realise until the end of 2018 that I suffered from aphasia. That explained why I became emotional when stressed and also hesitated to speak when conversing with more than one person.

Prior to the Chit Chat Café, there was no support group for those with aphasia and their caregivers. The primary focus of this programme is to help those with aphasia relearn basic communication skills through continual engagement, while also providing peer support for this poorly understood disability.

The person behind Chit Chat Café is Evelyn Khoo, who, in May 2019, decided to work independently from SNSA. SNSA has continued to organise aphasia programmes for its members under Move with Words. So, there are now two separate organisations in Singapore to help those with aphasia.

I found my role as a stroke advocate very fulfilling as I do corporate talks to share my experiences as a stroke survivor, ranging from talks in libraries, insurance talks, to allied health professionals as well as corporate staff welfare programmes. I did talks for SNSA on stroke awareness at companies and libraries. I shared my personal story of how stroke can be avoided as 1 in 4 people would get a stroke in their lifetime.

On 28 October 2021, I was humbled when I was asked to share my stroke journey at the 2021 World Stroke Congress via zoom. This was a liberating exercise.

Corporate talks *My talk held at Prudential Insurance*

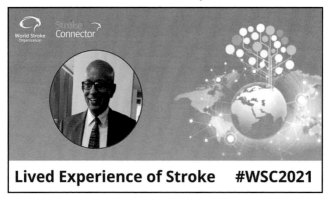

2021 World Stroke Congress Participant

Creating a Community of Speakers

Mindvalley is another organisation that has captured my attention. I have been following it since July 2018, and I like the way that CEO Vishen Lakhiani has built his organisation. Vishen is a former Malaysian Indian who is now settled in America. He is the author of *Code of the Extraordinary Mind*. I hope to work with Vishen to bring more events to Asia, particularly regarding how an empowered mind can bend reality in any direction. I have learned how their speakers have helped many people around the world, speakers like Gregg Braden, Donna Eden, and Bruce Lipton.

What I have learned through my journey and searches can be put to good use now that I would like to not only advocate for stroke recovery funding but also to build a community of stroke survivors so that more can gain from these illuminating digital platforms, just as I have from the likes of Vishen Lakhiani, Greg Braden, Donna Eden, and Bruce Lipton.

With technology digitised and so readily available, the multitude of technological benefits can now be shared amongst those stuck within four walls despite their physical and financial limitations. The digital platforms have now opened the possibilities for these otherwise unheard individuals who now are able to not only participate but also to listen to others with similar experiences and challenges. These platforms will encourage more to join and keep their stress at bay with support online, where participants can share their varied experiences and issues.

This noble cause forms the basis upon which we could seek to build ourselves, others, and our lives step-by-step. I hope to do Zoom seminars together with similar companies like Mindvalley and to set up a digital platform for all those with challenges. We could learn how to manage our current stages by keeping our stress at bay and allowing us to be motivated all through our lives.

CHAPTER 20

REALISATIONS

Life is an aspiration. Its mission is to strive after perfection, which is self-realization. The ideal must not be lowered because of our weaknesses or imperfections.

—Mahatma Gandhi[26]

When looking back over my life, I can say without hesitation that I would change nothing.

Do I live a life of regret? Do I groan over the loss, pain, and suffering? Do I mull over and feel pride for the many achievements in my life, ignoring other aspects? Do I simply remember the good that came my way and gloss over the bad?

My answer to all of those questions is a resounding 'no!' Never will I live in the past! The past is past! It is gone. I choose to live in the now and in the future, and that motivates me to push forward. My stroke left me with a vacuum and a new volume of time that I never had before. Time had come to a standstill, as if it had conspired with space to swap places. I once used to cover space whenever I travelled, and in my busy life, I tried to beat time.

I now have more time, and this book has filled that vacuum. Never once in my life did I think that I would actually write a book, but this book, *Stroke of Gratitude: How to Find Truth, Love and Happiness in Heal-*

ing After a Health Crisis, gave me a new purpose in life after 3 July 2012. With time finally on my side, I dived deep into my past to recall my long journey of life. I am amazed and humbled by my past—it sometimes even left me feeling numb. Memories flashed through my mind, and fleeting images surfaced of my childhood, family, friends, school life, work and my tumultuous yet exciting business milestones. During that time, so many people had come into my life for whom I am eternally grateful—Manjit Singh, Richard Ng, Christopher and Sharon Tan, S. H. Yusof, Abdullah Hameed, Jansen Wong, Arul Selvam, Adrian Chua, Michael Goh, Gerald Lim, Pushpa Tulsidas, and Josef Plattner, to name just a few.

As I embarked on my new journey of writing, I was shocked to learn how all-consuming my work life had become before my stroke. At 55, I realised that I had spent 60 percent of my life working—roughly 12,045 days where I primarily had one thing on my mind: my business. And we accomplished a lot. I transitioned from industrial cleaning to beauty and wellness, and now I have my sights set on helping the less fortunate.

In my younger days, I started doing business from a pay phone, and then, 29 years later, I was running a midsize enterprise with 450 staff and 10 business centres within Singapore. And it was not only myself who experienced success; a total of 13 spas were opened with my former staff members at the helm.

My persevering spirit drove me forward to expand my business regionally and once to become a major shareholder in a public company, then on the German and Australian securities exchanges. But I have difficulty recalling family life during those 29 years. It was Pathma who focused on raising our children at home, so I missed so much of their growing up years. That's why I cherished the time I spent with them bringing bags of local treats to St Joseph's Home, and my heart fills with joy when recalling the many drives to school with my daughters.

Much like the eagle that made the decision to adapt and survive, I chose to take painful steps to change my life so I could look back on my life with happiness. I feel such gratitude toward my family and friends who stood by my side and offered support after I suffered my stroke. Their encouragement lifted my spirit and made my journey as a stroke survivor so much more meaningful, especially during the daily uphill battle for my mind and my body.

As I endured the challenge and the pain of trying to heal my partially paralysed body and regain movement, I could relate to the eagle's painful struggle to shear its beak and pluck out its feathers and talons. My body wanted me to stop so many times, but my mind compelled me to keep going. I kept telling myself that I had nothing to lose and everything to gain. I had to exercise and follow through on my treatments to regain my strength, flexibility and mobility. Once I started to make improvements, it became much easier to enjoy the process and appreciate my progress, no matter how slowly it occurred.

I became totally driven to make myself stronger, and that helped me endure the many hours of speech therapy, physiotherapy, occupational therapy, Ayurvedic massages, biological cell regeneration therapies, Proslim therapies, vibration training, lymphatic drainage massages, qi-master biofeedback therapy, Bioresonance therapies, motivational CDs, SpinoFlex sessions, acupuncture sessions, stem cell therapies in Thailand, Ayurvedic camp in India, siddha treatments, countless Traditional Chinese Medicine (TCM) needles, and Varma massages, to name only some of the treatments.

The records and files documenting the daily, weekly, monthly and yearly hours I spent on my recovery now fill an entire cupboard. I have pictures and videos that depict the gruelling sweat-filled and pain-filled exercise and treatment sessions I endured to help me get where I am today. I'm reminded of how worthwhile the struggle was when friends who haven't seen me in years make remarks like 'You look much better, Aanandha!' and 'You have improved a lot!' It feels great when many of the taxi drivers who drove me back and forth to rehabilitation, meetings, seminars, and work remark on my progress. Those words of encouragement confirm that I am still moving in the right direction on my journey to recovery.

It was my determination and my indomitable spirit that always pushed me forward and further on my march to freedom and independence. I want to instil that same level of motivation in those who are facing similar challenges. My message to everyone is always believe in yourself and channel your spirit to overcome challenges and ultimately persevere. You will continue to make progress unless you stop, and stopping is the *only* way that you won't succeed.

This has been my eagle journey, and you may also be on your eagle journey or know someone who is. The journey of the mind is in no way prescriptive; it is up to each individual to choose their own path. When overcoming obstacles, facing challenges, and seeking oneself from within, each individual has to map out their own journey.

Anxiety and stress can be avoided if you know how to go around them. Approach life from the heart and not the brain. Analyse yourself. You are strong. You may not be aware of the many resources within you until you face a major life-changing challenge. The importance of sleep, exercise, and nutrition, with a proper lifestyle that balances work with good relationships, are indeed necessary for everyone to lead a good life.

Putting time aside to build strong bonds with family, friends and associates will ensure you operate from the heart and not just from the mind. When that happens, you will be happy, and the body will heal itself. This has not only helped me live an empowered life after my stroke; it can be used by anyone to navigate through life's challenges.

If I can help just one person to avoid a stroke, I will have accomplished my mission in writing this book.

CHAPTER 21

WE ARE ONE!

Individually, we are one drop. Together, we are an ocean.

—Ryunosuke Satoro

I didn't take my near-death experience lightly, and I didn't see it only as a drawback. It taught me how to be grateful for what I have, how to love more deeply, how to forgive more quickly, how to think higher thoughts, and how I needed to do more good in the world. It also taught me about the fragility of life. It taught me how my ego can convince me that I am invincible when, in reality, I'm just as vulnerable as anyone else. I could be here one moment and gone the next. That doesn't mean I can't make my mark, strive for greatness, and achieve the unachievable. Everything has a cycle, and everyone is in the same boat.

The real question is: Are we here to conquer the external world or the internal world? I had already attained my dream of becoming a high-achieving person in the world of business, but when that tower was struck down, I realised that my dreams were not built on the strongest of foundations. They were built on many false and limiting beliefs. But my near-death experience taught me that life is more about mastering the internal terrain of the mind—my emotions and learning how to create reality from within. Had I not fallen, I never would have broken through my own plateau of understanding the world and my relationship with it. I was given the chance to operate from a more genuine place in the heart.

If you can't manage your relationships, you are not going to be a torch for your family, friends and coworkers. They will avoid you, and you might not even understand why. In life, people find it easier to deal with people who are fluid, flexible and fun. This is why good things seem to happen to those who are happy or make others happy. Stormy moods, stubborn attitudes and sulkiness will not attract many happy things into your sphere. On the contrary, they will do the opposite and attract people who are held down by a lot of negativity.

Hoʻoponopono: Loving and Forgiving from Within

Hoʻoponopono is a process I learned to go deeper into healing by accepting full responsibility for what you are feeling and what is happening in your life. The term 'Hoʻoponopono' is a Hawaiian word that means 'making things right'. This Hawaiian forgiveness ritual is key to our life's fulfilment, it is well known for the miracles it does in clearing negativity from one's mind and thoughts. The four profound sentences that this forgiveness ritual include are 'I am sorry. Please forgive me. I love you. Thank you.'[27]

As Dr. Martin Luther King Jr said, 'Forgiveness is not an occasional act, it is a constant attitude.'[28] Learning to hear your inner voice and the universal voice is a lifelong process that provides a solution to our stress and life's turmoil. It is important to have the courage to see our mistakes and to show appreciation for what we have, and this will make the bonding stronger. Life is not about yourself but everyone and everything that is connected to you. It is necessary to see life as one beautiful chance given to you by God and to handle it with love. Live your life without grudges and be happy.

Koolulam: Oneness from within to All

Another interesting phenomenon that attracted me was something I had come across on 5 July 2020: Koolulam, established three years ago in Israel, is a social-musical initiative with a goal to strengthen society through mass singing events. Koolulam brings together people from all walks of life to do one thing—stop everything for a few hours and just sing together. This is a beautiful way whereby Koolulam inspires people from all religions to sing together as music will unite us as one.

When I heard about this Israeli social singing sensation that had a gathering of Jews, Christians, and Muslims in June 2018 at the Tower of David Museum in a vocal show of unity, coinciding with the Muslim holiday of Eid al-Fitr, it inspired me in the thought of oneness that brought everyone together in one space with a common goal to strengthen the fabric of society. This unique respect for each other's beliefs is so empowering, and it brings us together to yet another important factor: Mother Earth.

Care For Our Mother Earth: Being One with Nature for Our Common Good

We should also show more respect to our Earth. When we do this, it cultivates a form of self-respect within us. Even if you do not believe in climate change, you can appreciate how we all want to maintain a certain quality of life for ourselves and for future generations. We can always travel to another place, but if we don't change our ways, we will only find ourselves repeating the same mistakes and suffering from the same inner conflicts.

Our Earth is resilient, and given a chance, it will regenerate. We often think it needs saving, but consider that it may really be *us* who need saving. The regeneration process takes a long time, and it would be a pity if we lost all that we have right now simply because we lacked the foresight to make adjustments to our lifestyles. The more time we can buy, the more time we have to devise and test better solutions for everyone.

I cringe every time I hear that the rainforest and jungle have been replaced by pasture for cattle grazing. The deforested lands sustain cows for meat used in the hamburgers we eat at fast-food outlets as well as in our homes. On the vegan and vegetarian side of the spectrum, these lands are also being used to grow soybean crops and house palm oil plantations, which virtually wipe out the land's resources. The rainforest is able to regenerate itself, but its power is not unlimited; it dies after a 10-year soybean crop harvest. That is why it's important for everyone to begin eating less meat and also be conscious about how we transition into a greater demand for vegetarian and vegan-friendly options, so that the planet can return to balance.

I'm calling only for moderation and gradual, well-informed transitions. I'm calling for us to start making decisions from a place of conscious awareness, so we are more aware of *how* we make our decisions and what false beliefs are holding us back. When deciding what balance of meat and vegetables we would like for ourselves, ask how much it serves a real-life function as a transition for the planet versus being associated with a perceived moral high ground? Once we know where we stand, we can achieve inner peace, and our world will begin to naturally adjust with less struggle.

One way we can achieve inner peace and equilibrium is through mental visualisation techniques. Most days, I wake up and think: *If this were my last day on the planet, how would I like to spend it?* It helps me prioritise the important things in my life, such as having good relations with family, being productive, not wasting my time (or anyone else's), and also having some fun. I try to think more positively and provide measured solutions for problems. I first make sure my most basic needs are taken care of so that I can worry about other people's needs and then the planet's needs. If you don't take care of yourself first, it will be like trying to shine a light for others while standing in quicksand and stuck in the dark.

Visualisation helps me to live in the moment and be more in my heart and less in my head. Scientists have tested how many thoughts the average human mind processes every day. Can you guess the figure? It's between 30,000 and 70,000 thoughts per day. What percentage do you think are positive? If the results are to be believed, it appears that humanity has a long way to go. An estimated 80 percent of the thoughts produced by a human being every day are pessimistic.[29] So, how many of those thoughts have any real relevance or impact on our lives? That's why I make a conscious decision to choose optimism over pessimism. If you aren't an optimistic person yet, the good news is that we can all change.

Ever since I was a young student, I sought to establish myself in life. Every challenge I encountered along the way seemed like a mountain that needed to be climbed. Once I reached the top of each mountain, the one thing that propelled me to keep going was my belief in myself and in the universal force that we call God. When driven by this belief in God, it strengthened my faith in myself.

I remember my papa saying that all religions lead up to one almighty God. I believe that God sent messengers at different times in the history of man to serve the different needs of the time. It is only man who has created the divisions. My papa allowed us children to follow any faith we wished to, but it became increasingly clear to me that no matter which God you believe in, be it Krishna, Jesus, Buddha, Mohammad, Guru Nanak, or Hashem, faith will strengthen you to overcome great odds. That force beyond you will also nurture and guide you through calamities, like it did for me. The solace I found during my search to redefine myself kept leading me back to the same point: we are one!

When I began to explore the notion that we are one, I sought out others from different faiths to learn what messages they carried for humanity. It was a pathway to be taken with confidence and belief, but it had to be taken with small steps. I felt that no matter how long it would take, I would eventually make it, no matter what. When the realisation did arrive, it filled me with renewed confidence and a sense of calm. That sudden calm empowered me to think clearly, act with focus, and move at my own pace yet with determination. I was liberated, and challenges no longer felt like great obstacles.

What made me feel good was that only *I* needed to decide what that path should be. Nobody could dictate that. I needed only to listen to myself and not seek other opinions. I would know what that path would be when the time was right, and in the end, there was no right or wrong path. It was my journey to seek out the greater good that could guide me, and I felt the nature of the human spirit to be boundless. Once I came to that realisation, I became stronger and sought to challenge myself by further pushing beyond my physical limitations.

I reached a point where it didn't really matter where that nourishment or guidance came from as long as it served the greater good. Like the butterfly that breaks through its cocoon, struggling to be released, the human spirit has to journey through life's challenges, unhindered or helped by others, so that it benefits from self-realisation. When the truth is revealed, the spirit is healed, and it is happy. And that is what makes us all the same. No matter how different we are, or what lessons we learn along the way, we come out the same because we all seek the path toward truth, happiness, and healing.

This realisation is what left me thinking of my stroke as a gift in strange wrapping paper and provided me with a sense of calm. I looked back upon my stroke with gratitude because it made me who I became—nourished and empowered to soar to greater heights with a renewed passion, just like the eagle that regenerated itself. It took the eagle only six months. My journey, however, proved to be longer, but because of the support of my family, friends, and caregivers, it proved to be a fascinating journey filled with invaluable insights.

DALAI LAMA

Every day, think as you wake up,
today I am fortunate to have woken up.
I am alive.
I have a precious human life.
I am not going to waste it.
I am going to have kind thoughts toward others.
I am not going to get angry
or think badly about others.
I am going to benefit others
as much as I can.

ACKNOWLEDGEMENTS

I would like to thank Pathma Ananda, my wife, who stood behind me during these nine years to shoulder responsibilities that were previously mine. Her resoluteness and forbearance spurred me on to carry on and to finally finish this book. Great gratitude to Nishta Ananda and Triynka Ananda, my daughters, who saw me through this ordeal from July 2012, and I am proud of their achievements.

I would like to thank my mother, Savithiri Ratnam, for always believing in me. Her prayers were my constant blessing. She is the epitome of what a son hopes for in a mother.

I would like to thank my sisters, Sweeta, Rohini, Sharmini, Jassy, Anita, and my brother, Sri. Sri and Jeyathurai (Pathma's brother) were instrumental to us settling the case with Mayar in 2013. Without their financial assistance, advice, help and support we may not have been able to resolve this very difficult situation in my company and family life. Thank you to Pathma's mother, Mrs. Jeyalaxmi Durai, who passed on in 2014, for her constant support and prayers. She was the anchor for both the Ananda's and the Durai's families. Thank you to Pathma's sisters and brothers, Jayamalar, Viya, Vasanti, Shanti, Jeyathurai, Nirmala, and Maharaj and their spouses, Kumaresadas, Jennifer, Vijay, and Rain.

Thank you to Dr. Tang Kok Foo, a really great doctor, for his care in getting me out of a difficult life-and-death situation. Thanks to all the allied medical staff at Mt Elizabeth Hospital, especially Sivakumaar S. G., Hui Yong, and Dawn Bak.

Thank you, Dr. Zulia Frost from the United Kingdom, for your timely advice during my first few weeks of recovery.

Thank you, Dr. Darren Weissman and Trevor Gollagher, for the breakthroughs I received. Thank you, Dr. Darren, for the thoughtful foreword of this book. Thank you, Sharon Palmer, for all your advice on my genetics and my nutrition at the beginning of my recovery.

Thank you, Aunty Ann Selvarajah, who has been a very close family friend since 1960, and Aunty Rasamah Bhupalan, who was a constant adviser from my early teens.

Thank you to Manjit Singh who helped me get started in 1984 and has been a great support. How we enjoyed being involved in charity projects together! Thank you, Adrian Chua, S. Arulselvam, and S. H. Yusof for helping me get started at the beginning of Atos.

Thank you, Walter Joseph, for helping me to get to know Australia in 2006 and assisting me with my challenges to this day. I am filled with gratitude, as you were someone whom I could rely on at any time.

Thank you, Josef Plattner, for being my constant adviser between 2007 and 2010 as I went about running the public company in Australia.

Thank you, Mario and Mela Fiala from Vienna, for the very good training of our staff in my absence.

Thank you, Sekar Muniayappan, for starting me off on my journey with Varma Kalai massage. Thank you, Dada Ananyananda and Kulbhushan Kakar from India, for their time to look into my treatments.

Thank you, Raja Mohan and Greg Watters, for taking so much care with my recovery process—Raja with Varma Kalai massage and Greg with yoga and pranic healing. I so much enjoyed when we went swimming in the seas at Changi.

Thank you, Dr. A. Sundardas, for coaching me with Success Permissions that allowed me to reach my peak performance in business from 2009 to 2012.

Thank you, Vincent Yong, for showing me how dance can help me in the future. I enjoyed our stimulating discussions as well as SNSA sessions.

Thank you, Tan Bien Kiat, Arun Kemer, Rajagopal Babasankar, and Mirza Namazie, for your constant support during these nine years.

Thank you to the Atos team for looking after our customers these last nine years, especially Audrey Tan, Betty Sim, V. Asokan, Janis Tang, Kelly Yeo, and Malkit Kaur.

Thanks to the Singapore National Stroke Association (SNSA) for giving such great programmes that benefited me greatly. Special mention to Tan Poh Choo, Ann Tan, Associate Professor Deidre Anne De Silva , Dr. N. V. Ramani, Dr. Shamala Thilarajah, and Dr. Ng Wai May.

Thank you, AshvinDas, for ensuring that my insurance policy was taken before I had my stroke. Without that, I would not have been able to get the benefits of the various allied medical treatments while in hospital.

Thank you, Rudi Michelson from Melbourne, for patiently going through the manuscript and giving me valuable feedback.

Thank you to the Book Launchers team for helping me finish our book, especially CEO Julie Broad and Jaqueline Kyle.

APPENDIX 1

MING JYE

In a journal by Ming Jye, he cited that his secondary school life had not been a memorable one. He was often the target of insults '. When Ming Jye eventually completed his secondary education, he began making ends meet earning a meagre pay of only $300 per month at a game shop.

Just when life seemed set for Ming Jye, he met Aanandha.

Apprehensive at first, Ming Jye was extremely touched at how a total stranger was able to sympathise with him and willingly offered to help him without asking for anything in return. The extraordinary generosity and affection of Aanandha toward Ming Jye challenged his previous encounters. Weight problems are not only detrimental to physical health—they are even more so to a person's emotional health. Losing weight is not always about looking good but feeling good as well.

The journey was a long and arduous one, especially for one who was accustomed to an unhealthy diet throughout his life. But with sheer determination and will, accompanied by overwhelming support from the Atos team, Ming Jye successfully pushed onward toward a healthier lifestyle.

Other treatments that Ming Jye received included bioresonance metabolism booster therapy, Atos M3 vibration, Synergy, radio frequency fusion, InterX, manual lymphatic drainage, and Cellutrasson. All in all, Ming Jye has received benefits such as a whole-body detox from lymphatic drainage, steady and safe weight loss, and enhanced wellness from within, as well as a boost in metabolism to enhance energy burning.

What used to be his identity from the curves of his severely obese figure became a figment of the past as in 2011 Ming Jye stood at a tremendously improved weight of 86.6 kg from a previous 200 kg. His total circumference loss was a tremendous improvement of a 188.5 cm reduction.

A man whose confidence got repressed by the weight of his own body, Ming Jye was a living example of how devastating weight problems can be on a person's physical well-being as well as their emotional well-being.

'The people near me neglected me so much that I hated my life,' said Ming Jye.

The story of Ming Jye brings to mind how I met Ming Jye in 2008. I wanted to help him lose weight, and Ming Jye needed someone who believed that he could lose weight.

Just like I was the person who encouraged Ming Jye, I had many other people who really believed and encouraged me in my stroke recovery. I always knew that Atos could help people to lose weight with our treatments, exercise regime and encouragement. This had provided us with an opportunity to prove that.

Like Ming Jye, who was able to lose 114 kg in two and a half years, I know that after nine years I can see a slow but constant improvement in my physical condition, and I feel this is due to the numerous people who have been encouraging me onward.

VINCENT YONG,
CMA, RSME/T, BFA

Vincent Yong is an award-winning movement analyst, therapist, artist, speaker, and author. He is currently the only **certified movement analyst** (Laban/Bartenieff Institute of Movement Studies, LIMS) in Singapore and the only internationally conferred **registered somatic movement educator and therapist** in southeast Asia.

Holding **degrees** in dance (Codarts Hogeschool voor de Kunsten) and movement analysis (Laban/Bartenieff Institute of Movement Studies), Vincent is certified in a variety of somatic modalities such as the Laban Movement System, Bartenieff Fundamentals, and Body-Mind Dancing, and Moving For Life™, in which he was conferred **Cancer Exercise Specialist** by Dr. Martha Eddy (renowned somatics educator of the world).

RAJA MOHAN & GREG WATTERS USING VARMA KALAI THERAPY & YOGA

In my case, it was the near-death experience that brought me in contact with two special therapists. My stroke allowed me to cross paths with two healers—Raja Mohan and Greg Watters. Unbeknownst to me, they had also had their own brushes with death.

When I first met Raja Mohan, I asked him how he came across his unique healing modality, and this is what he said. Raja Mohan had parachuted hundreds of times. That day felt a bit different than the others, but although he was hesitant, he dismissed his uneasiness and continued to join his team in a routine parachute exercise above the jungle.

Raja Mohan remembers hitting the treetops at full speed and blacking out. The unthinkable had happened: both his primary and secondary parachutes had failed. He was presumed dead, but a rescue mission was launched, and a few days later he was found, barely breathing and unconscious on the jungle floor.

He was rushed back to Singapore for treatment and eventually moved to India for nine months to repair and rebuild the cracks and breaks to most of the bones on the right side of his body. In Tamil Nadu, he sought the services of a siddha medicine master to help him recover and also teach him Varma Kalai.

After nine months, Raja Mohan recovered, and he started to share with friends and family the great benefits of India's natural medicine system, the 'siddha way'. Soon after, he started to work with a brain development company in Singapore, helping autistic children and challenged kids to overcome their limitations using powerful siddha herbs and various techniques passed on to him from his many masters.

He regularly returns to India to spend time with his masters, who live deep in the rugged parts of the Himalayas of Tibet, Nepal, and India.

Some friends suggested this ancient Indian medicine technique as a way to accelerate my healing. Raja Mohan was recommended, so I set up a few appointments and within a few short weeks, I could feel a difference. My right-arm function, balance, and walking were the main areas we focused on, and they started to work better.

A few weeks after Raja Mohan started Varma Kalai therapy, he brought a friend along to one of our sessions—an Australian who was a yoga teacher, pranic healer, and Inner Power X instructor. Little did I know at the time that all three of us had experienced near-death experiences.

Greg was working in South America as a foreign correspondent for the Australian Broadcasting Corporation when he contracted typhoid. It took him three years to recover and turn his life around.

He started doing pranic healing for me and suggested some neurogenic yoga to help with my mobility and flexibility.

Once again, I noticed a vast change in my energy levels, mobility, mental clarity, and overall health. The three modalities of pranic healing, Varma, and neurogenic yoga helped me considerably.

In my heart of hearts, I know that if I had not crossed paths with these two healers, my recovery would have been slower.

Their dedication, research, and support has been invaluable in getting me to a better space and creating the shift in my life that was needed for me to rebuild. I am very grateful to both of them.

Not only did they help me heal myself; they shared information and worked out ways to help many other people achieve better health.

APPENDIX 4

SELECTED PROGRESS REPORTS

Appendix 4	Aanandha's Progress Reports
4A	Berg's Balance Assessment
4B	Exercise Assessment
4C	Muscle Power Assessment
4D	2017 Daily Exercise Report Summary
4E	2018 Daily Exercise Report Summary

4A: BERG'S BALANCE ASSESSMENT	14.04.15	25.01.16	01.08.17	01.08.17	15.08.17	08.09.17	12.09.17	03.11.17	26.1.18	05.04.18	16.10.18
1 **Sitting to Standing** (use armchair, feet shoulder width apart). Instruction: Please stand up. Try not to use hands for support.	4	4	4	4	4	4	4	4	4	4	4
2 **Standing unsupported** (feet shoulder width apart with arms folded across chest. If one UL is weak, hold it up with good UL against chest). Instruction: Stand for 2 minutes without holding	4	4	4	4	4	4	4	4	4	4	4
3 **Sitting unsupported** (feet on floor hands on lap. Feet together and well supported on the floor). Instruction: sit for 2 mins without holding.	4	4	4	4	4	4	4	4	4	4	4
4 **Standing to Sitting** feet shoulder width apart. Instruction: Please sit down.	4	4	4	4	4	4	4	4	4	4	4
5 **Transfer.** Instruction: move from chair to bed/chair and back again.	4	4	4	4	4	4	4	4	4	4	4
6 **Standing unsupported** with eyes closed. Instruction: close your eyes and stand still for 10 seconds.	4	4	4	4	4	4	4	4	4	4	4
7 **Standing unsupported with feet together** (feet together and arms across the chest). Instruction: stand with feet together for 1 minute without holding. 1.04 sec.	4	4	4	4	4	4	4	4	4	4	4
8 **Reaching Forward** with outstretched arm. Instruction: Lift arm to 90 degrees, stretch out your arm and reach forward as far as you can.	3	4	4	4	4	4	4	4	4	4	4
9 **Pick up object from the floor** (feet shoulder width apart. Place object 30 cm in front of toes. Use dominant or intact UL). Instruction: Pick up the shoe/slipper/keys on the floor in front of you.	4	4	4	4	4	4	4	4	4	4	4
10 **Turning to look behind over (L) & (R) shoulders,** (trunk must rotate). Instruction: turn to look behind you over towards left shoulder. Repeat to the right. 54 sec.	4	3	3	4	4	4	4	4	4	4	4
11 **Turn 360 degrees.** Instruction: Turn completely around in a full circle. Pause, then a circle in the opposite direction. Left Turn: 5.34sec.	2	2	2	2	2	2	2	2	2	2	2
12 **Placing Alternate foot on stool.** Place whole foot onto the step. Instruction: Place each foot alternately on the stool 4x as fast as you can without falling. 37 sec.	2	2	3	3	3	3	3	3	3	3	3
13 **Stand unsupported foot in front** Test both LL and take the lower score. Instruction: Place 1 foot directly in front of the other foot. If not, try to step far enough ahead so that the heel of the front is ahead of the toes of the back foot. RT in front: 1.04sec. LT in front : 26 sec.	3	1	4	4	3	3	4	4	4	4	4
14 **Standing on 1 leg** Test both LL and take the lower score. Instruction: Stand on 1 leg as long as you can without holding. Left leg: 38sec. Right leg: 0.56sec.	1	1	1	1	1	1	1	1	1	1	1
LL: Lower limb **UL:** Upper limb **T O T A L …**	47/ 56	47/ 56	49/ 56	50/ 56	49/ 56	49/ 56	50/ 56	50/ 56	50/ 56	50/ 56	50/ 56

: EXERCISE ASSESSMENT

NOFLEX/TREADMILL EXERCISES

EXERCISES	DURATION						
	02.08.17	15.08.17	08.09.17	12.09.17	03.11.17	05.04.18	16.10.18
Walking	10 min	10 min	10 min	10 min	10 min	10 min	10 min
Marching	2.11 sec	1.23 sec	1.08sec	1.06sec	1.27sec	1.27sec	1.44sec
Standing on Right leg	Average of 1.2sec	Average of 1.2sec	Average of 1.2sec	Average of 1.2sec	Average of 1sec 5ms	Average of 1min 36sec	Average of 1min 32sec
Standing on Left leg	Average of 15sec	Average of 31 sec	Average of 37.5sec	Average of 46sec	Average of 1m 12sec	Average of 1m 12sec	Average of 1m 12sec
Weight bearing Right	1.31 (set1) 2.0 (set 2)	52 (set1) 1.46 (set 2)	51sec(set1) 51sec(set2)	51sec(set1) 40(set2)	60 sec(set1) 56(set2)	46 sec(set1) 46 sec(set2)	52 sec(set1) 45 sec(set2)
Weight bearing Left	1.41sec(set1) 1.43sec(set2)	1.18sec(set1) 1.34sec(set2)	1.16sec(set1) 1.16sec(set2)	1.07sec(set1) 1.08sec(set2)	1.21sec(set1) 1.14sec(set2)	1.15sec(set1) 1.21sec(set2)	1.46sec(set1) 1.46sec(set2)

R EXERCISES

Squatting	1.22 sec	1.40sec	1.06sec	51sec	50sec	38sec	40sec
Marching	1.33sec	1.07sec	54sec	42sec	44sec	52sec	55sec
Weight bearing Right	56sec	59sec	51sec	47sec	49sec	44sec	46sec
Weight bearing Left	1.36sec	1.49sec	1.49sec	1.09sec	1.09sec	1.07sec	1.07sec
Leg swing side	1min	58sec	49sec	51sec	40sec	40sec	43sec
Leg swing front, back	56sec	54sec	1.13sec	1.11sec	1 min	50sec	1.05sec

EXERCISES

Knee extension both	1.09sec	59sec	45sec	32sec	53sec	32sec	57sec
Alternate extension	1.31sec	1.16sec	1.16sec	1.13sec	1.29sec	1m 30sec	1m 30sec
Knee bending	34sec	27sec	39sec	32sec	36sec	27sec	41sec
Right knee bending	1.10sec	23sec	28sec	26sec	29sec	24sec	33sec
Hand pull up	1.29sec	1.06sec	59sec	59sec	1.33sec	1 min	40sec
Chest/Biceps/Triceps	53sec	40sec	40sec	36sec	35sec	30sec	25sec
VAFIT STEPPER	100times -3.21sec	set 1: 100times - 2.44sec	set 1: 100times - 2.55sec	set 1: 100times - 3.02sec	set 1: 100times - 3 min	set 1: 100times - 3min 40sec	set 1: 100times - 2min 37sec
		set 2: 100times - 2.49sec	set 2: 100times - 3.16sec	set 2: 100times - 3.36sec	set 2: 100times - 3.02sec	set 2: 100times - couldn't do.	set 2: 100times - 2min 44sec
r -	Standing for 10min						

4C: MUSCLE POWER ASSESSMENT

JOINTS	MOVEMENTS	MUSCLE POWER						
		01.08.17	15.08.17	08.09.17	12.09.17	14.11.17	05.04.18	16.10.18
UPPER LIMB								
SHOULDER	Flexors	3+	3+	3+	3+	3+	3+	3+
	Extensors	3	3	3	3	3	3	3
	Adductors	3+	3+	3+	3+	3+	3+	3+
	Internal Rotators	3+	3+	3+	3+	3+	4	4
	External Rotators	2	2	2	3	3	4	4
ELBOW	Flexors	4+	4+	4+	4+	4+	4+	4+
	Extensors	3	3	3	3	3	3	3
RADIOULNAR JOINT	Supinators	2	2	2	2	2	1	1
	Pronators	1	1	1	1	1	1	1
WRIST / HAND	Flexors	3+	3+	3+	3+	3+	4+	4+
	Extensors	1	1	1	1	1	1	1
	Radial Deviators	2	2	2	2	1+	1+	1+
	Ulnar Deviators	2	2	2	2	1+	1+	1+
LOWER LIMB HIP	Flexors	3+	3+	3+	3+	3+	3+	3+
	Extensors	3	3	3	3	3	3	3
	Adductors	3+	3+	3+	3+	3+	3+	3+
	Internal Rotators	3+	3+	3+	3+	3+	3+	3+
	External Rotators	2	2	2	2	2	2+	2+
KNEE	Flexors	3+	3+	3+	3+	3+	3+	3+
	Extensors	3+	3+	4	4	4	4	4
ANKLE / FOOT	Plantar Flexors	2	2	2	2	2	3	3
	Dorsi Flexors	2	2	2	2	2	2	2
SUB TALAR	Evertors	1+	1+	1+	1+	1+	1+	1+
	Invertors	2	2	2	2	1+	2	1+

Muscle Power 1 - Flicker, no movement
Muscle Power 2 - Full range of movement in elimination of gravity
Muscle Power 3 - Full range of movement against gravity
Muscle Power 4 - Full range of movement against gravity with minimum resistance
Muscle Power 5 - Full range of movement against gravity with maximum resistance
Remarks: 14.11.17 While doing movement, felt more weak than before.

4D: DAILY EXERCISE REPORT 2017				
DAYS	**LL: LOWER LIMB EXERCISES**	**MODALITIES**	**UL: UPPER LIMB EXERCISES**	**MODALITIES**
MONDAY	Multi function + Stepper	Neuro move (shoulder, wrist,ankle)	In sitting, shrugging,use cane,resistance bands	InterX (Spine/ lower limb)
TUESDAY	Spinoflex	Proslim	Multi function (M3)	Balance exercises
WEDNESDAY	Bar exercises	BCR	H 200 / functional	InterX (lower limb/ Upper limb)
THURSDAY	Bar exercises	Proslim	Multi function (M3)	Co-ordination exercises
FRIDAY	Multi function + Stepper	Neuro move (shoulder, wrist,ankle)	In sitting, shrugging,use cane,resistance bands	Balance exercises
SATURDAY	Spinoflex	Proslim	H 200 / functional	InterX (Spine/ upper limb)
SUNDAY	Bar exercises	BCR	In sitting, shrugging,use cane,resistance bands	Co-ordination exercises

4E: DAILY EXERCISE PROTOCOL (2018)

DAYS	LL: LOWER LIMB EXERCISES	MODALITIES	UL: UPPER LIMB EXERCISES	MODALITIES	DURATION
MONDAY	Multi function (Lower limb)+ Stepper 45min	Neuro move (wrist,ankle) 30min	In sitting, shrugging,use cane 30min	InterX (Spine/Scalp) 30min	2hr 15min
TUESDAY	Spinoflex 45min	Proslim (Training/Relax) plan accordingly 60min	H 200 / functional 30min	Balance exercises (3 exercises) 30min	2hr 45min
WEDNESDAY	Bar exercises 45min	BCR 60min	Multi function (Upper limb) 30min	InterX (Upper limb) 30min	2hr 45min
THURSDAY	Multi function (Lower limb)+ Stepper 45min	Proslim (Training/Relax) plan accordingly 60min	Resistance bands/ Dumbells 30min	Co-ordination exercises(Heel toe gait, single line walking, back walk, side walk) 30min	2hr 45min
FRIDAY	Bed exercises 45min	Neuro move (wrist,ankle) 30min	Multi function (Upper limb) 30min	Balance exercises (3 exercises) 30min	2hr 15min
SATURDAY	Spinoflex 45min	Proslim (Training/Relax) plan accordingly 60min	H 200 / functional 30min	InterX (Lower limb) 30min	2hr 45min
SUNDAY	Bar exercises 45min	BCR 60min	Resistance bands/ Dumbells 30min	Co-ordination exercises (Heel toe gait, single line walking, back walk, side walk) 30min	2hr 45min

Note: Proslim
Training: Do training if Aanandha didn't do exercises for the whole day.

Endnotes

1   *The Love Letters of Mark Twain.* New York: Harper & Brothers, 1945, p.323.

2   Tendulkar, D. G. *Mahatma. Life of Mohandas Karamchand Gandhi...* 5. 2nd ed. Vol. 5. 8 vols. Delhi, India: Publications division of Ministry of Information and Broadcasting Government of India, 1960.

3   Tse, Lao. *Dao De Jing.* Translated by Keping Wang. Beijing, China: Foreign Languages Press, 2008.

4   Eliot, T.S. "East Coker." *Four Quartets.* Boston: Mariner Books, 1968, p.23.

5   Rowell, Rainbow. *Attachments.* New York: Plume, 2012.

6   Henry, Brad. "The Voter's Self Defense System." Vote Smart. Accessed September 30, 2021. https://justfacts.votesmart.org/public-statement/77474/governor-brad-henry-state-of-state-2005-transcript.

7   Anderson, Greg. *The 22 Non-Negotiable Laws of Wellness: Feel, Think, and Live Better than You Ever Thought Possible.* San Francisco: HarperSanFrancisco, 1996.

8   Rowling, J.K. "Harvard Commencement Address." J.K. Rowling, January 15, 2020. https://www.jkrowling.com/harvard-commencement-address/.

9   Mbella, Sango. *Sophia's Fire.* Spring City, PA: G&VPublishing, Inc., 2005, p.133.

10   der, Leeuw J J van. *The Conquest of Illusion.* Wheaton, IL: Theosophical Publishing House, 1966, p.9.

11   Kiyosaki, Robert T. *Rich Dad Poor Dad: What the Rich Teach Their Kids about Money That the Poor and Middle Class Do Not!* New York, NY: Perseus Distribution Services, 2017.

12   "10 Best Nature Quotes from Sir David Attenborough." WWF, May 6, 2020. https://www.wwf.org.au/news/blogs/10-best-nature-quotes-from-sir-david-attenborough#gs.co84zg.

13   Raja Mohan in discussion with the author.

14   Lipton, Bruce H. *The Biology of Belief: Unleashing the Power of Consciousness, Matter & Miracles.* Carlsbad, CA: Hay House, Inc., 2014.

15   Touillaud, Marina S., Anne C. M. Thiébaut, Agnès Fournier, Maryvonne Niravong, Marie-Christine Boutron-Ruault, and Françoise Clavel-Chapelon. "Dietary Lignan Intake and Postmenopausal Breast Cancer Risk by Estrogen and Progesterone Receptor Status." Oxford University Press, March 21, 2007. https://academic.oup.com/jnci/article/99/6/475/2522451.

16   "Shayne McClendon Quotes (Author of the Barter System)." Goodreads. Accessed October 1, 2021. https://www.goodreads.com/author/quotes/6534906.Shayne_McClendon.

17   Camus, Albert, and Justin O'Brien. *Notebooks, 1942-1951.* Chicago, IL: Ivan R Dee, 2010.

18   Kozlowski, Miroslaw, and Janina Marciak-Kozlowska. "Schumann resonance and brain waves: a quantum description." *NeuroQuantology: An Interdisciplinary Journal of Neuroscience and Quantum Physics* 13, no. 2 (2015): 196. *Gale Academic OneFile* (accessed September 30, 2021). https://link.gale.com/apps/doc/A462787551/AONE?u=anon~111473ac&sid=googleScholar&xid=9dc1bfef; Beason, Lori L. *Encyclopedia of the Human Brain.* Amsterdam: Acad. Press, 2002.

19   Tolle, Eckhart. *The Power of Now: A Guide to Spiritual Enlightenment.* Berkeley, CA: Distributed to the trade by Publishers Group West, 2004.

20   "Wizard Edison." *The Newark Advocate.* January 2, 1903, p.1.

21   Tracy, Brian. *Great Little Book on Mastering Your Time.* Mumbai: Jaico Pub. House, 2006.

22   "Singapore Stroke Registry Annual Report 2018 - NRDO." National Registry of Diseases Office, June 9, 2018. https://www.nrdo.gov.sg/docs/librariesprovider3/default-document-library/ssr-web-report-2018.pdf?sfvrsn=58eb7c4c_0.

23   Vincent Yong in discussion with the author

24   "Singapore National Stroke Association (SNSA) SNSA 2019 Annual Report." SNSA, December 31, 2019. http://www.snsa.org.sg/wp-content/uploads/2020/03/SNSA-Annual-Report-20199.pdf.

25   Wee, Elaine, ed. "Chit Chat Café a Stroke of Jazz - SNSA.ORG.SG." SNSA, September 2018. http://www.snsa.org.sg/wp-content/uploads/2019/04/StrokeWatch-Sept-to-Dec-2018.pdf.

26   Gandhi, Mahatma. *All Men Are Brothers: Autobiographical Reflections*. New York, NY: Continuum, 2004, p.91.

27   "Ho'oponopono: How to Practice It in 4 Simple Steps." Laughter Online University, December 6, 2018. https://www.laughteronlineuniversity.com/hooponopono-4-simple-steps/.

28   King, Martin Luther. *The Papers of Martin Luther King, Jr.. Advocate of the Social Gospel: September 1948 - March 1963*. Berkeley, CA: Univ. of California Press, 2007.

29   Rahmanov, Magsud. "80% Of Our Thoughts Are Negative - Control Them!" LinkedIn, March 9, 2018. https://www.linkedin.com/pulse/80-our-thoughts-negative-control-them-magsud-rahmanov/.